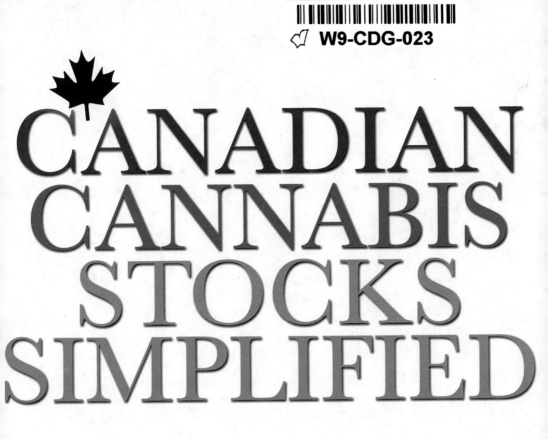

CANADIAN CANNABIS STOCKS SIMPLIFIED

CANADIAN CANNABIS STOCKS SIMPLIFIED

A How-To Guide for the Budding Investor

Corinne Doan MBA, BA

Self-Counsel Press
(a division of)
International Self-Counsel Press Ltd.
Canada   USA

Self-Counsel Press acknowledges the financial support of the Government of Canada for our publishing activities. Canadä

Printed in Canada.

First edition: 2018

Library and Archives Canada Cataloguing in Publication

Doan, Corinne, author

Canadian cannabis stocks simplified: a how-to guide for the budding investor / Corinne Doan, MBA.

(Self-Counsel business series)
Issued in print and electronic formats.

ISBN 978-1-77040-306-2 (softcover).—ISBN 978-1-77040-494-6 (EPUB).—ISBN 978-1-77040-495-3 (Kindle)

1. Stocks—Canada. 2. Investments—Canada. 3. Marijuana industry—Canada. I. Title. II. Series: Self-Counsel business series

HG5152.D63 2018	332.67'22	C2018-902178-0
		C2018-902179-9

Self-Counsel Press
(a division of)
International Self-Counsel Press Ltd.

Bellingham, WA	North Vancouver, BC
USA	Canada

Contents

Notice to Readers

Laws are constantly changing. Every effort is made to keep this publication as current as possible. However, the author, the publisher, and the vendor of this book make no representations or warranties regarding the outcome or the use to which the information in this book is put and are not assuming any liability for any claims, losses, or damages arising out of the use of this book. The reader should not rely on the author or the publisher of this book for any professional advice. Please be sure that you have the most recent edition.

Any data or information that is not directly cited in this publication is believed to come from reliable sources. This publication is not meant as a solicitation to buy or sell securities. Any recommendations are opinion only. At times, the writer may or may not own some of the securities discussed in the report. Cannabis is an emerging industry and, as such, the investment risks are high.

Acknowledgements

I'm grateful to have a support network of "honourary moms" and "besties."

Special thanks to Christine Musgrave. Thanks for your support hammering out my tag line, making sure I'm fed and housed, helping me run errands, all your care packages, and being an encouraging friend.

A very big thanks to Stephanie Halley for her perfect edits. You are a friend who could effortlessly and fluently translate "Cori speak" and contribute "budding" good ideas. After Stephanie read it, she said, "Seriously, you need to get this book published." With her approval, I knew I had something. Sadly, she passed away shortly after. I miss you, my friend.

Thanks to my landlord, George, for cutting me a smoking good deal on a great space to write this book. And thanks to another honourary mom who shares my name, for a place to crash while I continued my work. And for Monsieur Hodgson, my Grade 10 French teacher, I am more thankful than I can translate. Thank you for holding my hand and offering the "easy pitch."

I would like to thank and acknowledge Yvonne Turgeon from Before & After Media for the suggestion of marketing this book as a pre-edition. She also assisted a great deal in creating the graphics and website.

For publishing my book, I owe a debt of gratitude to Self-Counsel Press. Thank you for embracing this venture. And special thanks to my editor Eileen Velthuis and the rest of the team for elevating this book to its peak potential.

A sweeping thanks and gratitude to my extended family and friends for your ongoing support in getting me to this point. A very special thanks and debt of gratitude to every cannabis grow-op farmer, dealer, and customer who has risked their credibility and freedom for the past century.

On the note of those who have risked it all for cannabis I would like to give a special salute to Cheech and Chong. Cheech Marin and Tommy Chong are the most iconic characters associated with cannabis. Although known internationally, Tommy Chong is Canadian-born. The comedic duo, like Jerry Lewis and Dean Martin, or John Belushi and Dan Aykroyd, gained legendary status that will forever link one with the other. Cheech and Chong's careers hit a pinnacle with the 1978 movie *Up in Smoke*. The comedy followed two simple but lovable characters on their weed smoking adventures. Given the taboo subject of cannabis, the movie was financed inexpensively and was expected to gain a moderate return. However, the comedy was an unanticipated financial success ranking it the 15th highest grossing film of 1978 (Wikipedia, *Up in Smoke* (Wikipedia, accessed April 2018, https://en.wikipedia.org/wiki/Up_in_Smoke).

Despite being successful, the movie forever associated the actors/comedians with the illegal substance of marijuana. It was not Cheech and Chong's intention to be the beacon of the cannabis culture movement. They were just a couple of actors who were happy to have some success making people laugh. Cheech and Chong did not publicly endorse cannabis. Although, over the decades, they have posed the thought provoking questions, "What if we're right? What if marijuana is good for you?" (*Marijuana News*, "High in Hawaii: Cheech and Chong Talk Marijuana and Donald Trump" [420 Intel, 2016], accessed April 2018, http://420intel.com/articles/2016/05/06/high-hawaii-cheech-and-chong-talk-marijuana-and-donald-trump).

In real life, the actors found themselves persecuted by various legal authorities. Their personal characters were stigmatized and their careers stagnated. Chong tried to capitalize on his fame by financing and marketing a family run business which sold cannabis paraphernalia. During a US Attorney's drug operation, Chong's son was under investigation regarding their business. A violation of laws occurred when the "sting-like" operation requested a mail-order bong be sent to a fictitious town that was 31 miles beyond a county border. That county wasn't permitted to sell bongs. Tommy Chong took a plea deal in exchange for having all potential charges dropped against his son and wife.

Commencing October 2003, Chong was imprisoned for nine months plus was fined penalties of more than $100,000 USD. Of the 55 business owners that were investigated, Chong was the only one without a prior criminal record to receive jail time. Chong supporters (I amongst them) saw this as an unfair balance of justice. The tactics used were questionable, the law broken was minor, and the punishment was severe. The US Attorney's office justified the unusually harsh punishment by arguing Chong's fame to market the bongs and his finances to create the business made him a danger to children. In response, Chong said, "When they put me in jail, that's when they turned me into an activist. Up until the time I went to jail, I was just a comedian." (Brainy Quote, Tommy Chong Quotes [Brainy Quote, accessed April 2018], https://www.brainyquote.com/quotes/authors/t/tommy_chong.html).

In this book, I suggest the biggest challenge to the emerging cannabis industry is the undoing of 100 years of oppression and stigma. Mr. Chong's story is the perfect example. Since his imprisonment he has said, "To be in a situation where you have no rights whatsoever is something I wish everybody could experience. People's attitudes would change. It would be a better place."

Chong has found himself as an unwitting martyr and activist for the cannabis cause, and he has done it with grace and humour. I would like to thank him for the laughs. I am appreciative to count him a fellow Canadian. I'm beholden for his beacon. And I'm grateful Cheech and Chong have both lived long enough to be vindicated with their questions: "What if we're right? What if marijuana is good for you?"

Preface

Two decades ago, when I first started writing this book, it would have been illegal to write and prohibitive to discuss cannabis in many areas. The fact that laws have relaxed in Canada is delightful.

It is an unprecedented time, with an estimated $7 billion a year illegal industry (Health Canada, A Framework for The Legalization And Regulation Of Cannabis In Canada [Health Canada, December 2016]), about to be legalized across this country. Most analysts estimate this number could double in the first five years after legalization. The flood of money investing in legal cannabis operations is reminiscent of the Gold Rush era.

I'm a former stockbroker. My technical title was Investment Advisor. My first professional job was with McDermid St. Lawrence, which at the time was considered Canada's largest independent brokerage house. The firm's focus was venture capital underwritings for the oil and gas and mining sectors in Calgary, Alberta. I assisted three senior underwriters while managing my own client base. In addition to oil and gas and mining stocks, I was part of the tech boom years in the 1990s. I have experienced an inflated emerging industry and have witnessed roller coaster economic forces at work. I have also had the opportunity to wear many other hats during my career in the investment industry, including discount broker, investor relations, and compliance manager.

During my years as a discount broker, I became adept at explaining basic principles for stock trading to amateur investors. I used to keep a detailed list of the most popular customer questions. Next to the questions, I kept a tally of how many times each question had been asked. The data I collected established and verified the basic questions most asked by unsophisticated investors: This has formed the basis for this how-to book.

For decades, I have been close to a subversive culture of cannabis users during a sociopolitical climate of oppression, social stigma, and illegality. I have seen the blue collar working class fight the hardest battles around legitimizing cannabis. These were the grow op farmers, distributors, dealers, and consumers who risked their freedom and covertly contributed to what's been said to be a $7 billion annual industry.

My informal assessment is that most of these people do not have the experience or knowledge to make money on cannabis in the stock market. When I socialized with individuals in cannabis circles, I would find myself explaining how to buy cannabis stocks. Also, I heard complaints about it seeming unfair that sophisticated white-collar investors were reaping the profits from the road paved by the blue-collar working class. I realized I could help balance this unfair turn of events.

This book will help the budding investor who can afford to take some risks and wants to invest in cannabis stocks. Understand that risk means you may never get your investment back. Any investment in the cannabis industry is considered high risk. This is because all cannabis stocks are part of an emerging industry, and stocks in an emerging industry are brand new. Brand new stocks are venture stocks. Venture stocks are extremely high risk. There are no guarantees. New companies may come along; companies may close; some might change names and restructure along the way. There is risk. However, because it is a high-risk industry, it could mean great rewards.

This book is not intended to provide technical analysis for established day traders or sophisticated investors, though it would help them more effectively navigate the cannabis industry because I do list many publicly traded cannabis companies in Canada. I have also provided an independent thumbnail sketch analysis of the Licensed Producers (LPs) under Health Canada's new rules.

Also included are some investment strategies for consideration, and the manual intended to teach basic principles to trade stock.

Please note, all currencies are reflected in Canadian dollars unless otherwise specified.

Introduction

This book is a how-to investment guide for Canadian stocks associated to the emerging cannabis industry. Other investment self-help books explain a variety of subjects including penny stocks, OTC markets, day trading, budget planning, portfolio returns, and get rich strategies. As the Canadian cannabis market emerges, stock analysts are starting to write reports via investment newswires. Although a handful of books discuss American opportunities, until now it has been a challenge to find a Canadian cannabis stock book.

With all of this in mind, I have focused this book on two subjects: Canadian cannabis stocks, and tips for inexperienced investors. You don't need to be wealthy, educated, or sophisticated to benefit from this book. You just need the desire to take some risk to join the venture. I will cover the basic mechanics, to teach someone who has never entered a stock trade. I will also give you a road map to Canadian cannabis stocks that are currently available (at time of writing). These are the minimal tools required to invest in cannabis stocks. I'm gratified if this helps budding investors who need a few simple pointers to join in the "green rush."

1
Cannabis 101

1. What's in a Name?

It has been called marijuana, pot, ganja, bud, green, product, Mary Jane, wacky tabacky, Maui Wowie, herb, green, salad, weed; the list goes on. "Weed" is incorrect because cannabis is not a weed, it is a plant. The word "marijuana" is politically incorrect because it is a slang term which has racist connotations and origins. The word "cannabis" is Latin in origin and comes from ancient Greek.

Cannabis is the more appropriate term and is acceptable by today's social, political, and economic climate. Previously, those who have used cannabis have been labelled "stoners." This term has negative connotations and does not fairly reflect cannabis users. To neutralize the stigma of people who use cannabis, the suggested new politically correct term is to call the use of cannabis a "lifestyle choice."

2. Cannabis History

Cannabis has existed for as long as recorded history. The plant is indigenous to Asia and has been documented for more than 12,000 years. The Chinese recorded the use of cannabis as an anesthetic. It is listed as one of the 50 fundamental herbs in traditional Chinese medicine.

The cannabis leaf is prominently displayed in Egyptian art, and cannabis seeds have been found with mummies. There is evidence of it 2,000 years ago in India, where they called it ganja in ancient Sanskrit. The Vikings grew hemp for rope, but cannabis seeds have also been found with the remains of Viking females, suggesting they used them for medication.

It has previously been considered the fashionable narcotic of the upper class and amongst such, evidence suggests Shakespeare and Queen Victoria were users. Cannabis was a prominent part of western medicine, used as a pain reliever until the middle of the 19th century. Also, cannabis seeds were a staple in the world's diet until about the mid-1850s.

So how is it that in less than 200 years, a plant that was so much a part of a normal human life for tens of thousands of years was then declared an enemy on planet Earth?

The persecution of cannabis began at the turn of the 19th century. When cannabis seeds were brought to Latin America, the plant flourished. It was common for Mexicans to mix alcohol with cannabis consumption. When added to alcohol, cannabis increases inebriation. In the south western United States, racial tensions increased during the Mexican Revolution as immigrants crossed the border. The border itself was in dispute and some American land owners were on the losing side. The word marijuana began as a racist term that indicated an intoxicated Mexican who smokes cannabis. It became a term of social shaming and prejudice.

To control an unruly problem, the US was the first to prohibit cannabis, specifically in towns bordering Mexico in 1914. From there, powerful forces collided and merged with greed, arrogance, censorship, and ignorance to create an immense global movement. That's the nucleus to almost a century of worldwide persecution, prohibition, and oppression of cannabis.

North of the US border, Canada was having its own issues. It was a time of mass immigration for the developing nation. European immigrants were flocking to central Canada to farm and build railroads. Some brought alcohol. Chinese immigrants were flocking to western Canada to build railroads. Some brought opium. It was a volatile time for a young nation trying to find its way.

Despite well-documented problems with opioids and alcohol, a historian will struggle to find any evidence of issues with cannabis. The first attempts at substance control and prohibition were the

Canadian Temperance Acts of 1864 and 1878. The purpose of these Acts was to control alcohol. Thirty years later, the *Opium and Other Drugs Act* of 1911 was passed. The purpose was to control the opium drug dens in Canada's west.

The *War Measures Act* of 1914 allowed the provinces to enact alcohol prohibition. All provinces, with the exception of Prince Edward Island, repealed prohibition by 1924 and created the provincial alcohol control systems that are still in place today. While alcohol prohibition was being repealed, the *Opium and Other Drugs Act* was being amended to include opiate derivatives. Records show cannabis was not on any drafts of the bill amendment except the final. Other than mere notation by the Health Minister that cannabis was being added to the amendment there are no records to indicate who added it to the bill or why. In 1923, without any parliamentary debate, discussion, or consideration Canada was the first country to make cannabis illegal for an entire nation.

The *Opium and Narcotic Drug Act* was updated in 1929 and its penalties were severe. There was a provision for up to a 7-year prison sentence. In 1954, the penalty increased to a maximum 14 years in prison. In 1961, the *Narcotic Control Act* amended prison sentences as an indictable offence to a minimum of 14 years instead of a maximum.

Prime Minister Pierre Trudeau dared to challenge the cannabis prohibition. His government established The Le Dain Commission of Inquiry for Non-Medical Use of Drugs. In 1972, the commission recommended decriminalizing cannabis possession and allowing personal cultivation. A bill to remove cannabis from the *Narcotic Control Act* was passed by senate, but failed to pass the House of Commons. So, the laws remained unchanged. By the 1980s it was a crime to publish an opinion of cannabis punishable up to $300,000. This was challenged in court and ruled as a stifle to freedom of expression and therefore overturned in the Province of Ontario in 1994. In 1996, there was a change that saw the *Narcotic Control Act* repealed and replaced with the *Controlled Drugs and Substance Act* (CDSA). The Act decreased the penalties to six months of prison and/or a $1,000 fine for possession of up to 30 grams of cannabis.

In 2000, a court ruled Canadians had a constitutional right to medical cannabis, and in 2001 Canada became the first country to legalize cannabis for the terminally ill. The Medical Marihuana Access Regulations (MMAR) was created to establish legal access to patients from authorized producers. In 2013, this was changed to the Marihuana for Medical Purposes Regulations (MMPR) shifting focus from small local growers to large scale operations thus giving birth to the Licensed Producers (LPs). 2013 was also the year when British Columbia held a referendum to legalize cannabis. Also in 2013, federal Liberal leader Justin Trudeau announced his party platform which included the legalization of cannabis for recreational purposes. Trudeau won in 2015 and the MMPR was replaced by the Access to Cannabis for Medicinal Purposes Regulation (ACMPR) in 2016 which is paving the way for future changes.

Canada is a member of three international treaties that criminalize marijuana. As a sovereign nation, it may change its domestic laws. Canada has the right to withdraw from United Nations (UN) conventions after giving one-year notice. On April 20, 2016, the Canadian government announced at the UN its intentions to introduce legalization for recreational cannabis by spring of 2017. Other UN nations have changed their cannabis laws without sanction. Uruguay was the first nation to legalize recreational cannabis.

On April 13, 2017, the *Cannabis Act* was introduced to parliament. This time (as opposed to the previous attempt in 1972), it would seem there is enough incentive and momentum to pass this law. The house passed the third reading of the bill November 27, 2017 and sent it to senate. At the time of this writing, the senate had passed two of three readings. The suggested goal is to have recreational cannabis available in retail locations by summer 2018.

3. The Science of Cannabis

Cannabis is a plant with many unique and beneficial properties, which have been extremely difficult to verify. During the century of oppression, cannabis research was prohibitive. In the mid-1960s, a team in Israel dared to defy the global prohibition and conducted legitimate scientific research. Dr. Mechoulam is the scientist accredited for discovering cannabis's main active ingredient delta-9-tetrahydrocannabinol (THC). The field is new and emerging and the discoveries thus far are fascinating and encouraging.

3.1 Cannabinoids

Cannabinoids are chemical compounds secreted by cannabis plants. More than 60 cannabinoids and 600 compounds have been identified. These are the most discussed:

- THC delta-9-tetrahydocannabinol (THC) has properties that increase mental activity and stimulate appetite. It can be euphoric, muscle-relaxing, anti-epileptic, antiemetic, bronchial dilating, hypotensive, antidepressant, and an anesthetic. High- potency cannabis contains at least 15 percent THC.

- Cannabidiol (CBD) has sedative and analgesic effects.

- Cannabinol (CBN) is mildly psychoactive and aids in sleep and pain relief.

- Cannabigerol (CBG) has sedative and antibiotic effects, as well as acts to lower intraocular pressure.

- Cannabichromene (CBC) has mood-enhancing effects.

Cannabinoid receptors are sites throughout the brain and body to which cannabinoid binds. It was a significant breakthrough in scientific research in the mid-1980s when cannabinoid receptors were discovered in mammals, fish, reptiles, and birds.

Scientific research has concluded positive impacts from cannabis to help minimize seizures in humans with epilepsy. Cannabis has been clinically tested on children with cancer taking chemo treatment to help alleviate symptoms with positive results. Research also suggests that cannabis may be able to help reverse some effects of Alzheimer's and cancer, and is being studied in this regard. It has proven to be a powerful pain reliever, is an anti-inflammatory, relieves ocular pressure, and is antidepressant. That is just the beginning of the potential benefits of the cannabis plant.

There are two types of cannabis plants: sativa and indica as discussed in the next sections.

3.2 Terpenes

Terpenes are found in most plants and contribute to taste and smell. They may work with cannabinoids to attune our body's natural receptors.

3.3 Cannabis sativa

Sativa is the type of cannabis plant that is THC dominant. THC has stimulating properties. It is taller and lankier and characterized by short thin leaves. Its primary effects are that it is stimulating, uplifting, energizing, and is said to enhance creativity. Benefits are said to be that it reduces depression, relieves pain, reduces nausea, and stimulates appetite. Sativa is supposed to be generally good for daytime use.

3.4 Cannabis indica

Indica is the type of cannabis plant that is CBD dominant. CBD has sedative properties. Indica plants are normally shorter and stockier with wide leaves. Its primary effects are said to be stress and anxiety relief. Benefits are relaxation, sedation, pain reduction, sleep aid, reduction in inflammation, headache and migraine relief, reduction in nausea, and appetite stimulation. Indica is good for nighttime use.

3.5 Hybrid crosses

Hybrid crosses are the result of cross pollination of indica and sativa strains. Usually one strain will be dominant. Effects tend to reflect the dominant strain.

4. Cannabis Consumption

Cannabis needs to be heated above 120 degrees Celsius to activate the cannabinoids. There are two basic ways to consume cannabis: Inhalation or ingestion. Although, with a lesser degree of effectiveness, in a salve form, it also can be applied directly on skin to relieve aches and pains.

4.1 Smoking

Rolling a cigarette-style joint or using a pipe is the traditional form of inhaling cannabis into the lungs. Effects are felt immediately and may intensify for the first 20 minutes. Euphoric effects can last for a couple of hours, although some beneficial cannabinoids and terpenes can be destroyed in the combustion.

4.2 Vaporizers

Vaporizers are a tool used to inhale cannabis buds and oils. "Vaping" works like a mini-oven. Vaporizers will effectively release up to 95 percent of the cannabinoids and the effects are similar to those you would feel from smoking the cannabis.

4.3 Oils

Cannabis oil is a concentrated substance of THC and CBD created by extracting the active ingredients of the cannabis plant. Cannabis oil is efficiently digested by the stomach and liver. It takes the human body 30 to 90 minutes to feel the effects, which can last an hour or two longer than with smoking. Using a cannabis oil can be preferable to those who do not like to smoke or inhale cannabis. Also, the dosage can be more exact to maintain a consistent balance.

Oils can be administered with a droplet under the tongue or incorporated into edibles. Some producers flavour the oils with the essence of cinnamon, mint, lemon, coconut, etc., to make them more palatable for ingestion under the tongue.

Benefits to oil consumption are that the user is avoiding the harsh combustion intake of smoking, but more importantly, the ability to control the dosage of oils. There is no burning off of some of the beneficial compounds.

4.4 Edibles

Cannabis' active ingredients are extractable in fat and alcohol; from this, baked goods and tinctures can be produced. The stem of the plant which is commonly referred to as "shake," is less valuable for combustibles because it is less potent. But potency increases when cannabis is ingested thus making shake ideal for edibles. Shake is preferable for baking and may also be used to make tinctures and the stems for teas. The effects of edibles are similar to those of oils.

2
Cannabis Industry
Analysis of Investments

It is estimated there is a thriving market worth $7 billion dollars per year in illegal cannabis in Canada. That equates to roughly 700,000 kilograms of cannabis sold and consumed annually. Once cannabis is legalized, that number could double to $15 billion per year and some analysts say it will be higher. To put that in perspective, Canada had $9 billion in market sales for beer in 2015 (*National Post*, 2017, http://news.nationalpost.com/features/0-cannabis-retail-therapy, accessed April 2018).

The $7 billion projection is on target with the numbers experienced in the state of Colorado. Colorado voted to fully legalize cannabis in 2012. In January 2014, storefront locations were open for business. In year one, they had $700 million USD in sales. Within three years, sales were in excess of $1 billion with a population of 5.5 million. That confirms sales projections of approximately $1 billion for every 5 million people. With a population of 36 million people, Canada's projection is on target for cannabis sales to be $7 billion annually CAD or greater. This has a potential to increase as cannabis becomes more mainstream and accepted. Some analysts are projecting double, and some dare say triple this number over the next decade.

For the year 2016, approximately 20,000 kilograms of dried cannabis were legally harvested. That number is about to drastically change. Many of the facilities doing this work were not yet fully operational in 2016.

Virtually all the established producers have taken initiatives to expand their operations. The businesses that can produce the most cannabis will have the largest market share. Market share will impact stock prices. However, market share is not the only relative factor in a stock's price. Quality, reputation, and branding will also impact investors' decisions.

In the current cannabis industry climate, I am assessing three types of investments. These are the Licensed Producers (LP), the LP Applicants, and the ancillary. I have focused most of my analysis on the LPs. Also, I have provided a list of LP Applicants and ancillary stocks for your consideration.

This list represents my best efforts at the time of writing to be up-to-date and accurate; it is up to individual investors to research and do their due diligence for their investment choices.

1. Licensed Producers (LPs)

As of April 2, 2018, 97 cannabis businesses had been granted Licensed Producer (LP) status under the *Canada Health Act*. As of time of this writing, 55 LPs are publicly trading under 34 different companies. Initiatives have started to take more LPs public in the very near future. Also, some private LPs have sold portions of their interests to various medical and investment companies which are publicly trading. With mergers and acquisitions, the landscape of these investments is quickly evolving. See Table 1.

Next, Table 2 is a breakdown of all the Licensed Producers trading on Canadian stock exchanges. For this snapshot you will notice the company name, ticker symbol, the number of shares outstanding, the closing price and 52-week highs and lows, the known sizes of facilities, and the marketing budgets on a best efforts basis (at the time of writing).

Table 2 (along with much of the information in this book) is a living document in that the numbers are merely a snapshot of the

Table 1
The 97 Companies Currently Licensed to Produce Cannabis under Health Canada as LPs as of April 2, 2018

7Acres	James E. Wagner Cultivation
Abba Medix Corp.	KoLab Project
ABcann Medicinals	MariCann
AB Laboratories Inc.	MariCann (2nd site)
Acreage Pharms Ltd.	Medical Marijuana Group Corp.
AgMedica Bioscience Inc.	Medical Saints
Agrima Botanicals	MediPharm Labs
Agri-Médic ASP Inc.	Mediwanna
Agripharm Corp.	MedReleaf
Agro-Biotech Inc.	MedReleaf (2nd site)
Agro-Greens Natural Products Ltd.	Muskoka Grown Ltd.
Aleafia Inc.	Natura Naturals Inc.
Aphria	Natural Med
Aqualitas Inc.	Organigram
Aurora Cannabis Enterprises Inc.	Original BC Ltd.
Aurora Cannabis (2nd site)	PeaceNaturals
Aurora Cannabis (3rd site)	Potanicals Green Growers
BC Tweed Joint Venture Inc.	Prairie Plant Systems Inc.
Bedrocan Canada Inc.	Pure Sunfarms Canada Corp.
Bedrocan Canada Inc. (2nd site)	PureSinse Inc.
Beleave Kannabis Corp.	Quality Green Inc.
Bliss Co Holdings Ltd.	Radicle Medical Marijuana Inc.
Bloomera Inc.	Redecan
Bonify	Redecan (2nd site)
Breathing Green Solutions	Solace Health Inc.
Broken Coast Cannabis	Spectrum Cannabis Canada Ltd.
Canada's Island Garden	Starseed Medicinal Inc.
Canna Farms	Sundial Growers Inc.
CanniMed	Tantalus Labs
CannMart Inc.	THC BioMed Plant Science
CannTrust	THC Inc.
CannTrust (2nd site)	The Flowr Group (Okanagan) Inc.

Table 1 — Continued

Canveda Inc.	The Green Organic Dutchman
DelShen Therepeutics	Thrive Cannabis
Delta 9 Bio-Tech Inc.	Tilray
DOJA	Tweed Farms Inc.
Emblem	Tweed Grasslands Cannabis Inc.
Emerald Health Therapeutics	Tweed Main Street
Evergreen	United Greeneries
Experion Biotechnologies Inc.	UP Cannabis
FV Pharma Inc.	UP Cannabis (2nd site)
Green Relief	Vert Cannabis Inc.
Greenseal Cannabis Company Ltd.	WE Grow BC Ltd.
GreenEx Pharms Inc.	WeedMD
Hydropothecary Corp.	Whistler Medical Marijuana Corp.
HydRx Farms Ltd.	WILL Cannabis Group
Indivia Inc.	Zenabis
IsoCanMed Inc.	Zenabis (2nd site)

situation at the time of writing. Things can and will change so do your research if you are ready to consider investing.

2. Analyzing the Data

Analysts and sophisticated investors rely on a series of formulas and ratios to analyze financial statements to help influence their choices when deciding in what to invest. The ratios measure profitability, efficiency, liquidity, financial leverage, and shareholder return.

With emerging markets, revenues have not yet been established. Many of the new cannabis companies are not yet selling product so revenue cannot be adequately assessed. Most LPs that are selling product are still in their first year of sales, and revenue ratio analyses are skewed. Also, current sales are for medicinal purposes only and do not reflect the potential recreational market.

Therefore, most of the formulas used to determine the best potential investments are irrelevant and mean very little in emerging venture capital markets. Brokers are limited to looking for a company's ability to cover short-term debt obligations and market capitalization

Table 2
Licensed Producers Trading on Canadian Stock Exchanges

Licensed Producers Trading on Canadian Stock Exchanges	Ticker	Shares Outstanding in Millions	Previous Close CDN$ 04/02/2018	52-Week High	52-Week Low	Size of Facility in Square Feet	Marketing	Notes
ABCann Global	ABCN	187.59	1.59	4.06	0.80	29,000 to 500,000 could be 1,200,000	1,269,403	$204.8 million from 2017–Feb. 2018
Aleafia Health Inc.	ALEF	37.96	0.86	1.25	0.29	7,000 could be 1,200,000	764,974	
Aphria	APH	208.93	11.25	24.75	4.55	2,000,000	6,663,862	$255 million raised to Dec. 2017
Aurora Cannabis Inc.	ACB	490.04	9.07	15.20	1.90	1,190,000	10,270,000	$564 million from 2016–Jan. 2018
Beleave	BE	41.58	2.00	3.49	1.04	14,500 to be 200,000	609,149	$15 million in 2017
Benchmark Botanics	BBT	134.19	1.22	2.14	0.05	12,700 to add 50,000	not declared	
Bliss Co Holdings Ltd.	BLIS	99.59	0.46	0.76	0.07	unknown	5,291	
Canada House Wellness	CHV	116.38	0.26	0.90	0.13	49,500	578,195	$253,000 in 2017
Cannabis Wheaton	CBW	427.18	1.51	2.97	0.68	20,000 to 310,000 to be 1,900,000	not declared	$185 million from 2017–Jan. 2018
CanniMed Ltd.	CMED	24.76	34.15	46.00	7.32	247,000	4,096,000	$5.19 million in Jan. 2017
CannTrust Inc.	TRST	91.75	7.21	12.64	2.01	50,000 to be 480,000	198,858	$40 million in 2017
Canopy Growth	WEED	198.37	32.01	44	6.58	2,300,000 to be 5,645,000	23,452,000	$509 million from Dec. 2016–Jan. 2018

Table 2 — Continued

Licensed Producers Trading on Canadian Stock Exchanges	Ticker	Shares Outstanding in Millions	Previous Close CDN$ 04/02/2018	52-Week High	52-Week Low	Size of Facility in Square Feet	Marketing	Notes
Cronos Group	CRON	161.63	8.10	14.83	1.58	42,000 to be 353,000	not declared	$206 million from 2016–Mar. 2018
Delta 9 Cannabis Inc.	NINE	79.04	1.83	4.00	1.50	80,000 to be 272,000	not declared	$33.2 million in 2017
Emblem	EMC	104.65	1.38	3.38	1.30	23,500 to be 223,500	2,358,688	$185.55 million from Jan. 2017–Feb. 2018
Emerald Health Botanicals	EMH	121.47	4.75	9.68	1.06	4,000,000 calculated with splits from 6,900,000	428,541	$57.4 million from 2017–Feb. 2018
Golden Leaf Holdings	GLH	545.44	0.275	0.65	0.15	50,000	892,436	$52 million from 2017–Jan. 2018
Harvest One	HVT	149.25	0.90	2.20	0.47	16,000 to be 250,000	470,608	$100.25 million from 2017–Jan. 2018
HIKU	HIKU	131.14	2.09	4.82	0.44	7,100 to be 43,000	178,656	$39.5 million from 2017–Jan. 2018
Hydropothecary	THCX	179.19	3.86	5.25	1.10	36,000 to be 250,000 to be 1,000,000	2,986,424	$225 million from 2017–Jan. 2018
Indiva Inc.	NDVA	80.99	0.67	3.00	0.54	40,000	2,621	$36 million from 2017–Jan. 2018
Invictus MD Strategies	GENE	80.17	1.95	2.79	0.93	5,000 to be 140,830	2,079,584	$53.21 million raised in 2017
AIM1 Ventures	AIMI.P	9.48	0.32 halt	0.30	0.155	375,000	not declared	JWC is CGC craft grower
MariCann Inc.	MARI	73.41	1.82	4.48	1.05	44,000 to be 217,500 to be 630,000	2,630,990	$176 million from 2017–Jan. 2018

Table 2 — Continued

Licensed Producers Trading on Canadian Stock Exchanges	Ticker	Shares Outstanding in Millions	Previous Close CDN$ 04/02/2018	52-Week High	52-Week Low	Size of Facility in Square Feet	Marketing	Notes
MedReleaf Corp.	LEAF	99.99	16.93	31.25	6.81	55,000 to be 265,000	7,181,000	$257.5 million from 2017–Jan. 2018
Namaste Technologies	N	256.13	1.66	4.40	0.18	N/A	not declared	$35 million Feb. 2018
Newstrike Resources	HIP	482.38	1.12	3.30	0.27	24,000 to be 227,000	396,373	$100.1 million from 2017–Jan. 2018
Organigram	OGI	124.58	3.93	5.68	2.00	15,000 to be 429,000	2,846,938	$200 million from Dec. 2016 – Jan. 2018
Ravenquest BioMed	RQB	66.61	1.24	2.10	0.05	90,000	not declared	
The Supreme Cannabis Company	FIRE	250.01	1.68	3.49	0.98	342,000	513,455	$30 million Oct. 2017
Terrascend Corp.	TER	94.44	4.82	5.50	0.65	67,000 to add 40,000 to be 107,000	146,593	$56.5 million in 2017
THC Biomed Intl Ltd.	THC	116.41	1.58	3.36	0.295	unknown	41,761	$12 million in 2017
Viridium Pacific Group	VIR	46.07	1.03	1.75	0.18	8,300 to be 40,000	9,945	$3.8 million from Sept.–Nov. 2017
The Green Organic Dutchman	TGOD	6.10	0.00	0.00	0.00	970,000	not declared	$385.5 million from 2017– Mar. 2018
WeedMD Inc.	WMD	100.37	1.38	3.25	0.68	26,000 to be 610,000	not declared	$15 million Dec. 2017

or shares outstanding. They will also consider the company's reputation, which usually emphasizes looking at who is at the helm.

Other relevant factors are industry-specific. An oil, a gas, or a mining play might be more enticing if the location is close to an established fault line. Relevant factors for the cannabis industry are the size of the facility and brand recognition.

Let's discuss each of the companies listed in Table 2 in a little more detail, so you can assess the factors that might influence why you would or would not invest in certain cannabis stocks (again, this information changes frequently so look it up at the time of investing and make your own decisions).

ABCann Medicinals Inc.

Ticker: ABCN

Exchange: TSXV

Last trade: $1.59

> **52 week high:** $4.06
>
> **52 week low:** $0.80

Shares outstanding: 187.59

Location: Napanee, ON

Date of initial licensing: March 21, 2014

License type dry: Cultivation and sale

License type fresh oil: Production

Size of facility: 29,000 to be 150,000, could be 1,200,000

Marketing budget: $1,269,403

The stock commenced trading May 4, 2017. The company has raised approximately $205 million from 2017 to February 2018. ABCN acquired medicinal clinic Harvest Medicine for $1.5 million and 1.1 million shares in late 2017. ABCann has an extremely strong advisory board. Most noteworthy is Dr. Mechoulam who is considered "Father of Cannabis" for discovering delta-9-tetrahydocannabinol (THC) in the mid-1960s. Also on the board is Dr. Abrams who was on the front line of the AIDS crisis during the 1980s. He is now the Chief of Hematology-Oncology at San Francisco General Hospital. During my research, I have noted, these are the two most experienced, knowledgeable, and therefore referenced doctors in cannabis research worldwide. It is not possible to learn anything about cannabis without learning about the work of these two doctors. In addition, joining the board is Canadian business entrepreneur, billionaire, and former *Dragons' Den* dragon W. Brett Wilson. Wilson amassed his fortune in venture capital markets, specializing in the oil and gas industry. He brings an experienced business acumen that could be helpful in the emerging cannabis industry. Barry Fishman became the CEO in early September 2017.

ABCann claims to be organic and uses no pesticides. They don't require as much facility space because they only grow the plants to buds. The buds are extracted to be used in an inhaler as opposed to a vapourizer. With this technology, they project high yields of consistent product that works out to cost $10/gram for the customer.

The company has extended business interests in Germany, Australia, and Israel. ABCN accepted $30 million for building capital from Cannabis Wheaton (CBW) in exchange for future product at a discount rate. CBW is a cannabis streaming company with interests with 13 other partners. In late July, 2017, phase one commenced for a 100,000-square foot facility in Kimmet, ON. The adjacent land has enough room to expand to a 1.2-million-foot facility.

Aleafia Health Inc.

Ticker: ALEF

Exchange: TSXV

Last trade: $0.86

> **52 week high:** $1.25
>
> **52 week low:** $0.29

Shares outstanding: 37.96

Location: Scugog, ON

Date of initial licensing: October 13, 2017

License type dry: Cultivation

Size of facility: 7,000 square feet

Marketing budget: $764,974

Aleafia commenced trading with the ticker ALEF after a name change from Canabo Medical (CMM) in March 2018. The company also has dispensaries in ON, AB, and BC.

Aphria

Ticker: APH

Exchange: TSX

Last trade: $11.25

    52 week high: $24.75

    52 week low: $4.55

Shares outstanding: 208.93

Location: Leamington, ON, Vancouver and Cowichan Valley, BC

Date of initial licensing: March 24, 2014

License type dry: Cultivation and Sale

License type fresh oil: Production and Sale

Size of facility: 2 million square feet

Annual production: estimated 70,000 kg

Marketing budget: $ 6,663,862

With two million square feet, it aims to be amongst Canada's largest cannabis facilities. The company raised approximately $255 million in 2017. Aphria made an aggressive entrance to the US market when it invested $25 million in MMJs in Florida and Arizona. As cannabis remains illegal federally in the US, this action opened some precarious grey areas with financial regulations. In August 2017, the company asked the TMX regulators for clarity regarding American linked stocks. The TMX responded in October 2017, when it announced it would delist companies with US cannabis interests where cannabis remains federally illegal. This left a risk for APH. In the first quarter of 2018 APH announced intents to downsize and sell its American investments.

Also, in the first quarter of 2018 APH acquired 100 percent of LP Broken Coast based in British Columbia. Supply agreements were signed with Althea and Cannabis Wheaton (CBW:TSXV).

Aphria has entered an agreement to be a supplier for Shoppers Drug Mart, a Loblaw company. It was also awarded one of the supply agreements with the province of Quebec. At year end 2017, APH invested $10 million to the merger of Tokyo Smoke, and B.O.B. Headquarters with DOJA to create a new brand named HIKU. The merger with B.O.B.'s paid off when it won one of the four lucrative bids in Manitoba for retail cannabis stores in early 2018. The company has interests in Quebec with a joint distribution agreement with Tetra Bio Pharm. A further major supply agreement was signed in July 2017, with Scientus Pharma, a Health Canada licensed dealer. Aphria also invested $11.5 million with Scientus Pharma and Hydrx Farms.

Toronto-based Nuuvera Corp. bought the land across the street from Aphria to build a 1-million-square-foot facility. Aphria, in turn, bought $2 million in shares of Nuuvera. The intent will be to create a sum total of 2 million square feet under Aphria's LP license for joint cannabis operations. Aprhria acquired Nuuvera for $826 million in the first quarter of 2018. Nuuvera has business interests in Europe, Africa, and the Middle East. Nuuvera was renamed Aphria International.

Until recently, the town of Leamington was considered the Tomato Capital of Canada. Heinz Ketchup, which was in operation since 1909 closed its Leamington doors in 2017 resulting in a dramatic economic downturn for the area. As a result, the community has welcomed the emergence of a new use for their greenhouse facilities. The Tomato Capital of Canada may now become the cannabis capital of the world.

Aurora Cannabis

Ticker: ACB

Exchange: TSX

Last trade: $9.07

52 week high: $15.20

52 week low: $1.90

Shares outstanding: 490.04

Location: Cremona and Edmonton, AB; Pointe Claire and Lachute, QC; Saskatoon, SK; and interests in BC

Date of initial licensing: February 17, 2015

License type dry: Cultivation and Sale

License type fresh oil: Production and Sale

Number of registered patients: 19,000

Size of facility: 1,190,000 square feet combined

Annual production: 100,000

Marketing budget: $10,270,000

This Alberta-based Licensed Producer (LP) opened its first facility in Cremona, Alberta which they call Aurora Mountain. It is a 55,000 square foot facility. ACB is constructing a second facility named Aurora Sky, which will be 800,000 square feet next to the Edmonton airport. The location was a strategic choice to be able to ship orders internationally. It will be able to grow an estimated 100,000 kilograms per year. Aurora has been granted one of six licenses in

Quebec. The company has bought a 40,000-square foot facility in Pointe Claire named Aurora Vie. The company has also invested in a 48,000-square foot facility in Lachute, Quebec, which is a late-stage applicant. ACB has also acquired BC applicants Northern Lights BC and Urban Cultivator.

In the first quarter of 2018 ACB announced a partnership with a Danish tomato producer to set up production facilities to supply markets in Denmark, Sweden, Norway, Finland, Italy, and Iceland through its Aurora Nordic Cannabis branch. In January ACB became a cornerstone investor in LP Green Organic Dutchman for a stake in the company's equity plus a supply agreement. The investment was $55 million. In February 2018, ACB announced an agreement with Liquor Stores NA to develop a Western Canadian Retail Cannabis Business. ACB invested $103.5 million for the venture. Also in February 2018, ACB was awarded supply agreements for the province of Quebec and Shoppers Drug Mart.

The year 2017 was an active year, when ACB partnered with and acquired 19.18 percent of Radient MAP technology (RTI:TSXV) to specialize in cannabis oil extraction. ACB has also acquired 19.9 percent of Cann Group, which is a licensed company in Australia. In May the company acquired German wholesaler, exporter, and distributor for medicinal cannabis Pedanios for $13.6 million. In June 2017, ACB made a strategic investment for 19.9 percent with a 50 percent option in Hempco (HEMP), an established hemp seed provider. In September 2017, the company announced an agreement with Namaste (N:CSE), a vapourizer manufacturing company, as a hardware supply company. Namaste has since become an LP. In November 2017, ACB acquired greenhouse design firm Larsen Ltd. and H2 Biopharma. In December 2017, a letter of intent was signed with CannaRoyalty (CRZ:CSE) for international drug delivery technology. Also in December, a non-binding term sheet collaboration agreement was signed with Micron Waste Technologies (MWM:CSE). Micron is a developer of proprietary digester solutions for the treatment of organic waste.

In late November 2017 Aurora gained attention for its intention for a hostile takeover of CanniMed (CMED-TSX). CMED is Canada's first licensed producer based in Saskatoon, Saskatchewan. It operates two facilities which, combined, are 247,000 square feet. In response, CanniMed announced intentions to acquire Newstrike (HIP-TSXV). By acquiring HIP, CMED would be diluting its stock. By diluting its stock, it would make it more difficult for ACB to acquire CMED. This is what stockbrokers call a "poison pill."

The companies were forced to take their conflict to regulators. Rulings were made by the Ontario Securities commission and The Consumer Affairs Authority of Saskatchewan. A legal threat was made when CMED filed a $725 million lawsuit against Aurora. Calmer heads prevailed when in January 2018, CMED consented to a friendly take over bid for $1.1 billion. The deal was finalized in late March 2018. At time of writing CMED is still trading; it should be delisted by the time this book is published.

ACB had the prestigious graduation to the "big board" TSX on July 24, 2017. On November 28, 2017, ACB announced it had completed $115 million financing. Another $200 million bought deal was completed in January 2018. The company has raised more than half a billion dollars over the past three years.

Beleave Inc.

Ticker: BE

Exchange: CSE

Last trade: $2.00

52 week high: $3.49

52 week low: $1.04

Shares outstanding: 39.67

Location: Hamilton, ON

Date of initial licensing: May 18, 2017

License type dry: Cultivation

License type fresh oil: Production

Size of facility: 14,500 to be 200,000 square feet

Marketing budget: $609,149

The current facility is 14,500 feet with plans underway to expand to 60,000 then 200,000 square feet. The company raised approximately $15 million in 2017. Cannabis Wheaton (CBW-TSXV) is a financer with a $5 million Debt Obligation repayable in Product Equivalents (D.O.P.E. note) with the option for $5 million more. In late November 2017, the company announced $10 million financing.

Benchmark Botanicals

Ticker: BBT

Exchange: CSE

Last trade: $1.22

    52 week high: $2.14

    52 week low: $0.05

Shares outstanding: 134.19

Location: Peachland, BC

Date of initial licensing: October 13, 2017

License type dry: Cultivation

Size of facility: 12,700 to be 50,000 square feet

Marketing budget: unknown

Benchmark Botanicals owns LP Potanicals Green Growers.

Bliss Co Holding Ltd.

Ticker: BLIS

Exchange: CSE

Last trade: $0.46

    52 week high: $0.76

    52 week low: $0.07

Shares outstanding: 99.59

Location: Langley, BC

Date of initial licensing: March 29, 2018

License type dry: Cultivation

Size of facility: unknown

Marketing budget: $5,291

Bliss has signed an agreement to supply The Supreme Cannabis Company (FIRE:TSXV) with 3,000 kg of cannabis by June 2020.

Canada House Wellness Group

Ticker: CHV

Exchange: CSE

Last trade: $0.26

    52 week high: $0.90

    52 week low: $0.13

Shares outstanding: 116.38

Location: Pickering, ON

Date of initial licensing: September 1, 2017

License type dry: Cultivation

Size of facility: 49,500

Marketing budget: $578,195

Canada House Wellness Group owns LP AbbaMedix. The company closed a $253,000 financing in the summer of 2017 and is currently working on another financing. At year end they had a definitive joint venture agreement to manufacture cannabis oil extracts and cannabis infused products. The agreement is a 50/50 partnership for CHV to house the facility for Nutritional High International (EAT:CSE).

Cannabis Wheaton

Ticker: CBW

Exchange: TSXV

Last trade: $1.51

> **52 week high:** $2.97
>
> **52 week low:** $0.68

Shares outstanding: 427.18

Location: Carleton Place, ON

Date of initial licensing: August 25, 2017

License type dry: Cultivation

Size of facility: 20,000 and JV for 310,000 to be 1,900,000 square feet

Annual production: 200,000,000 gram

Marketing budget: unknown

Cannabis Wheaton (CBW) owns 100 percent of LP Kolab (formerly Rock Garden). With only 20,000 square feet it would seem a small company but CBW has further joint venture interests with FV Pharma, Cannabis Co, and Peter Quiring which would give the company interests up to 1.9 million square feet. CBW launched as a "streaming" company that invests in reciprocal agreements of money in exchange for future products. They created the D.O.P.E note which stands for Debt Obligation repayable in Product Equivalents. It has signed agreements with Abcann (ABCN:TSXV), Beleave (BE:CSE), and Aphria (APH:TSX). Further agreements have been signed with LP applicant Sundial and beverage maker Province Brands. The company has raised approximately $200 million since inception.

CanniMed

Ticker: CMED

Exchange: TSX

Last trade: $34.15

> **52 week high:** $46.00
>
> **52 week low:** $7.32

Shares outstanding: 24.76

Location: Saskatoon, SK

Date of initial licensing: September 19, 2013

License type dry: Cultivation and Sale

License type fresh oil: Production and Sale

Number of registered patients: 20,000

Size of facility: 247,000 square feet

Annual production: 16,000 kg/year

Marketing budget: $4,096,000

CanniMed is a wholly owned subsidiary of Prairie Plant Systems. The company has been growing medicinal cannabis for the government of Canada since the year 2000. It has two LP facilities with CanniMed and Prairie Plant. CanniMed holds the license to sell and Prairie Plant holds the license to cultivate and produce. The company closed a $5.19 million financing on January 30, 2017. In March it entered a distribution agreement with Pharmachoice. Further distribution agreements have been made with the Cayman Islands and Australia. A supply agreement was signed with Akula, a company trading in South Africa. In October 2017 the company signed an agreement with Avaria Health and Beauty for medicinal distribution.

In November 2017, CMED became newsworthy when it became the target for a hostile takeover from Aurora Cannabis (ACB-TSX). In response, CMED defended itself with by adopting a "poison pill." (A poison pill is a defense strategy against a hostile takeover.) CanniMed announced intentions to acquire Newstrike (HIP-TSXV). By acquiring HIP, CMED would be diluting its stock. By diluting its stock, it would make it more difficult for ACB to acquire CMED. The companies were forced to take their conflict to the regulators. In late December 2017, the Ontario Securities commission and The Consumer Affairs Authority of Saskatchewan ruled favourably for Aurora. In 2018, CanniMed agreed to the takeover. The deal was finalized in late March of 2018. At time of writing, the company is still trading, but should be delisted by the time this book is published. I note it as remarkable that a company which raised $5 million over the past year sold for a record $1.1 billion.

Cann Trust Inc.

    Ticker: TRST

    Exchange: TSX

    Last trade: $7.21

        52 week high $12.64

        52 week low: $2.01

    Shares outstanding: 91.75

    Location: Vaughan, ON

    Date of initial licensing: June 12, 2014

    License type dry: Cultivation and Sale

    License type fresh oil: Production and Sale

    Number of registered patients: 39,000

    Size of facility: 50,000 to be 480,000 square feet

    Annual production: to be 40,000 kg

    Marketing budget: $198,858

CannTrust commenced trading midsummer 2017 on the CSE. By the first quarter of 2018 it was trading on the TSX. The company has completed $40 million in financings in 2017. Their operating facility in Vaughan, Ontario is 50,000 square feet. In October 2017 the company was granted a second License Producer permit for a facility in the Niagara region. The Niagara facility is currently operating with 250,000 square feet and had its first harvest in December 2017. There are plans to expand the Niagara facility to 430,000 square feet. The company announced plans under consideration to expand to more than 1,000,000 square feet.

CannTrust Holdings also owns 50 percent of Cannabis Coffee & Tea Pod Company, a JV with Club Coffee, LP. The companies have received a patent with respect to single-serve containers for use in brewing a cannabis-based beverage and have licensed the IP to Lighthouse Strategies for use in Arizona, California, Colorado, Nevada, Oregon, and Washington. BrewBud is a US-patented unit dose pod formulation allowing the administration of cannabis single-serve brewing pods for use in Keurig, Nespresso, and Tassimo type brewers. In November 2017, Health Canada granted the company a license to export to Australia. In March of 2018 TRST expanded its stake with a joint venture with Denmark's Stenocare.

Canopy Growth Corp.

Ticker: WEED

Exchange: TSX

Last trade: $32.01

    52 week high: $44.00

    52 week low: $6.58

Shares outstanding: 198.37

Location: LPs in ON and SK with applicants in BC, NB, QC, NL, and AB

Date of initial licensing: November 2013

License type dry: Cultivation and Sale

License type fresh oil: Production and Sale

Number of registered patients: 29,000

Size of facility: 2.3 to be 5,645,000 million square feet

Annual production: 11,000

Marketing budget: $23,452,000

Canopy Growth Corp. (WEED:TSX), commonly referred as CGC, has become Canada's most well-known cannabis company and has been the trailblazer for others to follow. It was the first cannabis company to trade publicly in Canada. It began with the brand name Tweed; it merged and acquired eight LPs to form Canopy Growth. Tweed 1 and 2 (Smith Falls, ON), Bedrocan 1 and 2 (Toronto, ON), Starseed Medicinal, Spectrum Cannabis, (Bowmanville, ON), Agri-pharm (Clearview, ON), and Tweed Grasslands (Yorkton, SK) are all LPs who have merged to become Canopy Growth.

WEED has also bought LP Applicants. Spot Therapeutics in Fredericton, New Brunswick, with a 100,000-square-foot facility. An MOU was signed to build a 160,000-square foot facility named Sweet Grass in Edmonton. WEED has expanded interests applicant BC Bud to become BC Tweed, a 1.3 million square foot facility with the option to build 1.7 million more to be constructed in the Lower Mainland.

In September of 2017, WEED was able to secure one of two permits who will be the official supplier for the province of Newfoundland. WEED also has a strategic relationship for business in Quebec. In

November 2017, CGC bought interest in LP Terrascend (TER-CSE) for $52 million. Also, Canopy has announced an agreement to acquire intellectual property rights from Green Hemp Industries in Saskatchewan.

CGC has signed craft grower agreements to secure all their production for the CGC Mainstreet retail line. To date, nine growers have committed including AB Laboratories, JWC Ltd. Island Garden, Puff Ventures (PUF-CSE), Pheinmed (UMB-CSE), Valens GrowWorks (VGW-CSE), and Delta Nine (NINE-TSXV). With partnership with NINE, WEED has secured a distribution channel by winning one of the four bids for the Manitoba retail market. In the first quarter of 2018 WEED secured supply agreements with the provinces of Prince Edward Island and Quebec.

WEED has partnered with Snoop Dogg to establish international brand recognition through celebrity representation. Canopy has an exportation deal with MedCann GmbH Pharma and Nutraceuticals in Germany and has applied for a license in Australia. With Spectrum Cannabis Denmark there are plans for a 40,000 square meter facility in Odense. Through Bedrocan, there is an agreement with Brazil's Entourage Phyto Lab. Another deal in place with Australia's AusCann Group. In September 2017, WEED announced a strategic relationship with Spain by signing a supply license agreement with Alcaber Sa, a pharmaceutical company. Further international interests are in Chile. Also in September 2017, CGC signed a deal with Skinvisible Pharmaceuticals, an R&D company with a patented drug-delivery system topical formula. In October, a strategic partnership was formed with Jamaica-based Grow House. In November 2017, an agreement was signed with Farm to Farma; CGC has exclusive rights to manufacture and distribute Farm to Farma's Trokie® throat lozenges. A joint venture was announced with CGC and Colorado-based Oregna Brands and Netherlands-based Green House.

Approximately $509 million has been raised over the past three years. Quite possibly the most notable deal of the year and the benchmark for others to follow was the merging of the world's biggest cannabis company with one of the world's largest liquor conglomerates. On October 30, 2017, Canopy announced a $245 million investment for 10 percent of CGC by Constellation Brands. The international liquor company is most known for producing Corona beer. This was followed by a second event when Bank of Montreal (BMO) was the first major bank to invest in the cannabis industry when BMO invested $200 million in WEED.

WEED continues to look for venture opportunities with its Canopy Rivers division. Rivers is a streaming revenue sharing process with $20 million allocated to financing more ventures. In late December 2017, Rivers announced a joint venture agreement with Les Vert Cannabis to form a new company St Hane Bertrand Canopy Growth. Canopy has invested $15 million cash and 2.75 million shares to retrofit Les Serres tomato and pepper greenhouses.

Cronos Group

Ticker CRON

Exchange: TSXV and NASDAQ

Last trade: $8.10

52 week high: $14.83

52 week low: $1.58

Shares outstanding: 161.63

Location: Stayner, ON; and Armstrong, BC

Date of initial licensing: October 13, 2013

License type dry: Cultivation and Sale

License type fresh oil: Production and Sale

Size of facility: 42,000 to be 353,000 square feet

Annual production: 2,600

Marketing budget: unknown

Cronos Group made history when it became the first cannabis company to trade on a US stock exchange. On February 26, 2018 it commenced trading on the NASDAQ with a new ticker symbol: CRON. CRON began as a merchant bank which bought 100 percent of two Licensed Producers. Peace Naturals is operating in Stayner, Ontario. Original BC is a facility under development in Armstrong, British Columbia. Cronos also owns interest in three other LPs and one LP applicant. Cronos owns 21.5 percent of LP Whistler Medical in British Columbia, 6 percent of LP Abcann in Ontario, and 1.9 percent of the only LP in Quebec: Hydropothecary. Cronos also has an agreement to acquire 25 percent of LP Evergreen in Victoria, British Columbia. Cronos has further diversified interests with a joint venture agreement with Indigenous Roots to work with First Nations. In January 2018 the company received a Dealer's License under Health Canada. The company has announced a strategic relationship with a 45,000-square foot facility in Israel, and in November the TSX gave approval for Cronos Israel. Distribution agreements have been signed with Germany and Switzerland. At year end 2017, the company announced a successful first shipment to Pohl-Boskamp, a pharmaceutical manufacturer with distribution to 12,000 pharmacies in Germany. Med Men is a leading US-based company in California, New York, and Nevada; it entered an agreement to enter the Canadian market via Cronos. CRON is the second company (Canopy was first) to benefit from a bought deal from BMO for $100 million. BMO is the first bank to invest in the cannabis industry before legalization.

The company has raised approximately $206 million from 2016 through March, 2018.

Delta 9

Ticker: NINE

Exchange: TSXV

Last trade: $1.83

    52 week high: $4.00

    52 week low: $1.50

Shares outstanding: 79.04

Location: Winnipeg, MB

Date of initial licensing: March 18, 2014

License type dry: Cultivation and Sale

Number of registered patients: 2000

Size of facility: 80,000 to be 272,000 square feet

Annual production: 4,500 to be 18,900 kgs

Marketing budget: unknown

Delta 9 is one of two LPs based in Manitoba. This father/son team started operations in 2009. The company commenced trading on the TSXV on November 6, 2017, after a $5.2 million financing at $0.65/unit. The company had successfully raised approximately $33.2 million by the end of 2017. In November 2017, the company announced plans to expand its facility with the use of retrofitted container pods. Each pod offers 320 square feet and they plan to have more than 600 pods by 2020. Delta 9 became the ninth company to join Canopy Growth (WEED-TSX) as a craft grower. In the first quarter of 2018, NINE announced a strategic partnership with Westleaf Cannabis. Westleaf is based in Calgary and has interests in a Saskatchewan facility. NINE was a successful bidder for one of the four recreational sales permits in Manitoba. In March 2018, NINE signed an agreement with Fort Gary Brewing Company to jointly produce a hemp beer. Also in March, 2018, a letter of intent was signed to export cannabis to Kalapa of Germany.

Emblem Corp.

   Ticker: EMC

   Exchange: TSXV

   Last trade: $1.38

      52 week high: $3.38

      52 week low: $1.30

   Shares outstanding: 104.65

   Location: Paris, ON

   Date of initial licensing: August 25, 2015

   License type dry: Cultivation and Sale

   License type fresh oil: Production and Sale

   Number of registered patients: 2,091

   Size of facility: 23,500 to be 223,500

   Annual production: 12,000 kg/year

   Marketing budget: $2,358,688

Emblem is part of a larger integrated healthcare company called KindCann Holdings Ltd., that encompasses patient and physician education centers known as GrowWise Health. In May 2017, the company acquired land to build 2 x 100,000-square-foot facilities. In October 2017, an agreement was announced with Canntab Therapeutics for the development of an oral sustained release formulation. An agreement was signed at year end 2017 with Dosecann to develop a cannabis dosage-controlled formulation. In March 2018, EMC signed a supply agreement with Shoppers Drug Mart. The company has raised approximately $135 million from 2017 through February 2018.

Emerald Health

   Ticker: EMH

   Exchange: TSXV

   Last trade: $4.75

      52 week high: $9.68

      52 week low: $1.06

   Shares outstanding: 121.47

Location: Victoria, Delta, Vancouver, and Richmond, BC

Date of initial licensing: February 5, 2014

License type dry: Cultivation and Sale

License type fresh oil: Production and Sale

Size of facility: 4,000,000 calculated from 6,900,000 million with splits with VFF and Pure Sunfarms

Annual production: 150,000 kg/year

Marketing budget: $428,541

Emerald Health has three approved LP facilities. The first is based in Victoria. The second is a joint venture for a large greenhouse with Village Farms International (VFF-TSX). Village will contribute $20 million for 50 percent proceeds of a 1.1 million square-foot greenhouse in Delta, British Columbia. EMH to contribute the same $20 million to receive the same 50 percent. There is an option for the two companies to expand this facility to 4.8 million square feet. The third facility in Richmond is 75,000 square feet, to be expanded to 1.1 million square feet. This is another joint venture facility with Pure Sun farms which will receive 50 percent.

Also EMH has another applicant pending. A Metro Vancouver facility is 500,000 square feet with plans to be 1 million square feet. At time of writing this is an indicated total of more than 6.9 million square feet under EMH's Health Canada permit, of which the company has interest in the production profits of more than 2 million square feet and could be more than 4 million in the near future.

EMH acquired shares in Vanc Pharmaceuticals in late November 2017. At year end it was announced that EMH's subsidiary Northern Vine Labs and Abattis Bioceuticals (ATT:CSE) were granted an amendment to its Health Canada dealer's license. The company has the ability to transport, deliver, and sell product to other licensed dealers and licensed producers. EMH raised approximately $60 million from 2017 through February 2018.

Golden Leaf Holdings

Ticker: GLH

Exchange: CSE

Last trade: $0.275

    52 week high: $0.65

    52 week low: $0.15

Shares outstanding: 545.44

Location: St. Thomas, ON

Date of initial licensing: November 24, 2017

License type dry: Cultivation

Size of facility: 50,000

Marketing budget: $892,436

Golden Leaf owns LP Medical Marijuana Group Corp. GLH is based in Portland, Oregon, where it is a cannabis oil solution provider throughout North America. It has raised approximately $52 million from 2017 through January 2018.

Harvest One

Ticker: HVT

Exchange: TSXV

Last trade: $0.90

    52 week high: $2.20

    52 week low: $0.47

Shares outstanding: 149.25

Location: Salt Spring Island, BC

Date of initial licensing: June 28, 2016

License type dry: Cultivation and Sale

Size of facility: 16,000 (to be 250,000) square feet

Marketing budget: $470,608

Harvest One is the parent company of LP United Greeneries. The company commenced trading April 28, 2017. On May 1 2017, the company announced an agreement with Pann Cann to participate in financing and building of a facility in Lucky Lake in exchange for future equity participation. In November 2017, the company announced a strategic collaboration with e-Sense Labs Ltd. At year end 2017 the company announced a binding purchase agreement with United Greeneries for 398 acres of land in British Columbia. The purchase is in anticipation of amendments to regulations to accommodate for outdoor farms should they be allowed in the future. HVT has raised more than $100 million from 2017 through Jan 2018.

HIKU Cannabis Company

Ticker: HIKU

Exchange: CSE
Last trade: $2.09
> **52 week high:** $4.82
> **52 week low:** $0.44
Shares outstanding: 131.14
Location: West Kelowna, BC
Date of initial licensing: June 16, 2017
License type dry: Cultivation
Size of facility: 7,100 to be 43,000
Marketing budget: $178,656

This company originally named DOJA, commenced trading in August 2017. Trent and Rita Kitsch, founders of Saxx Underwear, own 33.33 percent of the shares. DOJA merged with Tokyo Smoke to form the new company Hiku. The deal was enhanced with a $10 million financing from Aphria (APH:TSX). Tokyo Smoke had recently merged with B.O.B. Headquarters based in Brandon, Manitoba. B.O.B. Headquarters was one of the four successful bidders to be permitted to operate retail store fronts in Manitoba. HIKU has made other strategic relationships by acquiring a Quebec design brand Maitri Group. In early 2018 HIKU acquired a stake in a Jamaican Medical cannabis firm, Kaya Inc. In March 2018, HIKU signed deals with Vitalis Extraction Company and announced a collaboration with an American-based company. The company raised approximately $40 million from 2017 until the end of January 2018.

Hydropothecary

> **Ticker:** THC.X
> **Exchange:** TSXV
> **Last trade:** $3.86
> > **52 week high:** $5.25
> > **52 week low:** $1.10
> **Shares outstanding:** 179.19
> **Location:** Gatineau, QC
> **Date of initial licensing:** March 14, 2014
> **License type dry:** Cultivation and Sale
> **License type fresh oil:** Production and Sale
> **Size of facility:** 36,000 to be 250,000 to be 1,000,000 square feet

Annual production: 108,000 kgs

Marketing budget: $2,986,424

This is one of Quebec's only six LPs, which is a small amount of LPs when considering the province's population respectively. On May 2, 2017, a voluntary recall was issued after Health Canada found low levels of containments. In July 2017, it announced a new product line using a mouth spray. The company signed a supply agreement with the Société des alcools du Québec (SAQ) on Valentine's day 2018. It was one of six companies to be awarded Quebec contracts. In March 2018, THCX announced it has chosen Shopify to power its e-commerce markets.

Indiva

Ticker: NDVA

Exchange: TSXV

Last trade: $0.67

    52 week high: $3.00

    52 week low: $0.54

Shares outstanding: 80.99 million

Location: London, ON

Date of initial licensing: July 14, 2017

License type dry: Cultivation

Size of facility: 40,000 square feet

Annual production: 300 to be 3,000 kg

Marketing budget: $2,621

Indiva commenced trading on December 19, 2017. Two days later it signed a supply agreement with a Swiss Cannabis producer. The company had raised approximately $36 million by the end of January 2018.

Invictus

Ticker: GENE

Exchange: TSXV

Last trade: $1.95

    52 week high: $2.79

    52 week low: $0.93

Shares outstanding: 80.17

Location: Hamilton, ON

Date of initial licensing: October 21, 2016

License type dry: Cultivation and Sale

Size of facility: 5,000 to be 166,000 square feet

Annual production: 5,000 kgs

Marketing budget: $2,079,584

Invictus acquired 100 percent of Acreage Pharms, an LP in Peers, Alberta. The facility will be 100,000 square feet. It also owns 50 percent of LP AB Laboratories in Hamilton, Ontario. It has signed a letter of intent to acquire LP applicant Plan C Biopharm. Plan C has a 60,000-square-foot facility in Salmo, British Columbia. I have noted Invictus is the only company to transparently reflect in detail its selling and marketing expenses on its balance sheets. In March 2018, Invictus gained some attention when it signed classic rock and roll personality Gene Simmons as its Chief Evangelical Officer. The company changed its stock ticker symbol to GENE to reflect its new brand. Approximately $53 million was raised in 2017.

James E. Wagner Cultivation

Ticker: AIMI.P

Exchange: TSXV

Last trade: $0.32 halt

    52 week high: $.32

    52 week low: $0.155

Shares outstanding: 9.48

Location: Kitchener, ON

Date of initial licensing: January 10, 2017

License type dry: Cultivation

Size of facility: 375,000

AIM1 Ventures announced a reverse take over in January, 2018 for LP James E. Wagner Cultivation (JWC). At time of writing the stock has not completed its closing transaction to commence trading. I suspect it will be relisted with a new ticker symbol. JWC is a craft grower for Canopy Growth (WEED:TSX).

MariCann Inc.

> **Ticker:** MARI
>
> **Exchange:** CSE
>
> **Last trade:** $1.82
>
> > **52 week high:** $4.48
> >
> > **52 week low:** $1.05
>
> **Shares outstanding:** 73.41
>
> **Location:** Hamilton, ON
>
> **Date of initial licensing:** March 27, 2014
>
> **License type dry:** Cultivation and Sale
>
> **License type fresh oil:** Production and Sale
>
> **Number of registered patients:** 11,000
>
> **Size of facility:** 44,000 to be 217,500 to be 630,000
>
> **Marketing budget:** $2,630,990

MARI has two LP permits. The first facility is 44,000 square feet. The second is to be 217,500. There are plans to extend this facility to 630,000 square feet. It has applied for a license in Germany to build a 1.5 million-square-foot facility in Dresden. In October 2017, the company acquired a biotech company with rights to a number of globally patented technologies that provide drug delivery formulations. NanoLeaf, through its licensing agreement with Vesifact, has developed and marketed the first cannabinoid standardized dose soft gel capsule. In November 2017, MARI announced it received a license from Health Canada to produce cannabis oil capsules. Also, in November 2017, MARI signed a letter of intent with Lovell Drugs. MARI is utilizing an automated software to network connectivity to streamline communication between process control functions, building automation, and material handling. This system offers an integrated plant-wide platform for process automation, environmental monitoring, and building management. In the first quarter of 2018, the company announced intent to acquire Swiss cannabis grower Haxxon. This Hamilton, Ontario-based company has raised approximately $176 million from 2017 to January 2018.

MedReleaf Corp.

> **Ticker:** LEAF
>
> **Exchange:** TSX

Last trade: $16.93

    52 week high: $31.25

    52 week low: $6.81

Shares outstanding: 99.99

Location: Bradford, ON

Date of initial licensing: February 14, 2014

License type dry: Cultivation and Sale

License type fresh oil: Production and Sale

Size of facility: 55,000 to be 265,000 square feet

Marketing budget: $7,181,000

MedReleaf commenced trading on the TSX in early June 2017. The company holds two LP permits. Both facilities are in Bradford, Ontario. The first is 55,000 square feet. The second is 210,000 for a combined total of 265,000 square feet. It signed a distribution agreement with CannaKorp during the summer. In September 2017, the company announced a research and development collaboration with Flora Fontica, a cannabis grow lighting specialty company. LEAF is the first company to offer a topical cream. The company made news at the end of 2017 after signing a supply agreement with Shoppers Drug Mart to sell medicinal cannabis online. In the first quarter of 2018, the company signed a supply agreement with the province of Quebec, received a Health Canada approval to produce cannabis oil soft gel capsules, and it commenced its operations in Australia. It also signed deals with Woodstock Cannabis for branding rights and a supply agreement with Cannamedical Pharma in Germany. It has raised approximately $225 million from 2017 to January 2018.

Namaste Technologies

    Ticker: N

    Exchange: CSE

    Last trade: $1.66

        52 week high: $4.40

        52 week low: $0.18

    Shares outstanding: 256.13

    Location: Toronto, ON

    Date of initial licensing: March 16, 2018

License type dry: Production

License type fresh oil: Production

Marketing budget: unknown

Namaste began as a manufacturer and distributor of vapourizers. The company signed a hardware supply agreement with Aurora (ACB:TSX) in the third quarter of 2017. In December of 2017 a strategic letter of intent was signed between Supreme Cannabis (FIRE:TSXV) and its wholly owned subsidiary LP 7Acres, with Namaste and its wholly owned subsidiary CannMart. The arrangement will allow Supreme to sell its product via Namaste's channels. Further supply agreements were signed with Phvida and ISOL in January 2018. In March 2018, CannMart made history when Health Canada permitted production licenses that are administered with the Licensed Producers. If and when they receive a sales license, CannMart will operate as one of the first aggregators of medical cannabis.

Newstrike Resources Ltd.

Ticker: HIP

Exchange: TSXV

Last trade: $1.12

52 week high: $3.30

52 week low: $0.27

Shares outstanding: 482.38

Location: Brantford, ON

Date of initial licensing: December 19, 2016

License type dry: Cultivation and Sale

License type fresh oil: Production

Size of facility: 227,000 square feet

Annual production: 12,000 kgs

Marketing budget: $396,373

Newstrike acquired LP UP Cannabis from Hemisphere Pharmaceuticals in Brantford, Ontario. They commenced trading on the TSXV on June 1, 2017. Newstrike has partnered with the popular Canadian rock band The Tragically Hip. Although not a marketing relationship, it is noted the chosen ticker symbol is HIP. Canadian entrepreneur W. Brett Wilson also divulged being a partner prior to the listing transaction. Up Cannabis has a 14,000-square-foot facility in Brantford and a 10,000-square-foot facility in Creemore, Ontario. The company is making a bid to acquire a 203,000-square-foot greenhouse facility in Beamsville, Ontario.

HIP gained attention in November 2017, when Aurora Cannabis (ACB-TSX) announced intentions for a hostile takeover of CanniMed (CMED-TSX). In response, CanniMed announced intentions to acquire Newstrike Resources (HIP-TSXV). By acquiring HIP, CMED would be diluting its stock. By diluting its stock, it would make it more difficult for ACB to acquire CMED. This is what stockbrokers call a "poison pill." The companies were forced to take their conflict to the regulators. In January 2018, CMED withdrew its takeover bid of HIP and agreed to a friendly takeover by ACB. HIP received $14 million from CMED to terminate its takeover. The same day, HIP announced $51 million financing. The company has raised approximately $100 million from 2017 to January 2018.

Organigram

Ticker: OGI

Exchange: TSXV

Last trade: $3.93

   52 week high: $5.68

   52 week low: $2.00

Shares outstanding: 124.58

Location: Moncton, NB

Date of initial licensing: March 26, 2014

License type dry: Cultivation and Sale

License type fresh oil: Production and Sale

Size of facility: 15,000 to be 429,000 square feet

Annual production: 4,200 (to be 65,000) kgs

Marketing budget: $2,846,938

This cannabis company claims an organic niche. At the end of the year 2016, the company had a product recall due to contamination. On March 29, 2017, Health Canada renewed OGI's license. In September 2017, the company entered an MOU to use a microwave extraction technique. The company has raised approximately $200 million from 2017 to January 2018.

Ravenquest BioMed

Ticker: RQB

Exchange: CSE

Last trade: $1.24

> **52 week high:** $2.10
>
> **52 week low:** $0.05

Shares outstanding: 66.61

Location: Markham, ON

Date of initial licensing: November 10, 2017

License type dry: Cultivation

Size of facility: 55,000 to be 90,000 square feet

Annual production: 11,000

Marketing budget: unknown

Ravenquest (RQB) has acquired 100 percent of LP Bloomera in Markham, Ontario. It has also invested in LP applicants Alberta Green Biotech in Edmonton and a First Nations facility in Fort Mc-Murray, Alberta.

The Supreme Cannabis Company

Ticker: FIRE

Exchange: TSXV

Last trade: $1.68

> **52 week high:** $3.49
>
> **52 week low:** $0.98

Shares outstanding: 251.01

Location: Kincardine, ON

Date of initial licensing: March 11, 2016

License type dry: Cultivation and Sale

Size of facility: 342,000 square feet

Marketing budget: $513.455

Supreme has acquired LP 7Acres. The company's focus is a B2B niche. In November 2017, Supreme signed a letter of intent with Alliance Beverage. Supreme made two strategic moves at the end of the year. The first was to purchase six acres of property adjacent to its current facility. The same day it was announced a letter of intent was signed for a supply agreement with Namaste (N:CSE). Namaste is a vapourizer manufacturing company turned LP with a wholly owned subsidiary CannMart, which is a marketplace for medicinal cannabis. FIRE raised approximately $30 million in 2017.

Terrascend Corp

Ticker: TER

Exchange: CSE

Last trade: $4.82

    52 week high: $5.50

    52 week low: $0.65

Shares outstanding: 94.44

Location: Mississauga, ON

Date of initial licensing: July 10, 2017

License type dry: Cultivation and Sale

Size of facility: 67,000 to be 107,000 square feet

Marketing budget: $146.593

Terrascend acquired LP Solace Health Inc. Canopy Growth (WEED:TSX) made a strategic transaction in TER acquiring 47.73 million shares with a $52.5 million investment.

THC BioMed

Ticker: THC

Exchange: CSE

Last trade: $1.58

    52 week high: $3.36

    52 week low: $0.30

Shares outstanding: 116.41

Location: Kelowna, BC

Date of initial licensing: February 18, 2016

License type dry: Cultivation and Sale

License type fresh oil: Production and Sale

Size of facility: Unknown (top secret, I have asked many times)

Annual production: 400 kgs

Marketing budget: $41,761

THC's facility is located strategically close to the Kelowna, British Columbia airport. THC has a niche marketing focusing on B2B shipping for clone plants. The company acquired Clone Shipper for $1 million USD in May 2017. Clone Shipper is an innovative technology to safely ship plants within a few days. At year end the company announced intentions to buy greenhouses in Ontario. It would give THC 100,000 square feet combined with its Kelowna operation and the possibility for an expansion to 300,000 square feet. The company raised approximately $12 million in 2017.

The Green Organic Dutchman

Ticker: possibly TGOD

Shares outstanding:: 6.1 million

Location: Ancaster, ON

Date of initial licensing: August 17, 2016

License type dry: Cultivation and Sale

Size of facility: 970,000 square feet

Annual production: 11,000 kg to be 116,000

Marketing budget: unknown

The Green Organic Dutchman (TGOD) facility is based in Ancaster, Ontario. The company has announced a second location in Salaberry-de-Valleyfield, Quebec. In January 2018 the company raised $112 million of which Aurora (ACB:TSX) became a cornerstone investor with $55 million in exchange for future production. On March 14, 2018, the company filed a $75-$100 million prospectus at $3.65/ unit. At the time of writing, the company is not yet trading.

Viridium Pacific Group

Ticker: VIR

Exchange: TSXV

Last trade: $1.03

    52 week high: $1.75

    52 week low: $0.18

Shares outstanding: 46.07

Location: Mission, BC

Date of initial licensing: August 18, 2017

License type dry: Cultivation

Size of facility: 8,300 to be 40,000

Marketing budget: $9,945

Viridium commenced trading on October 6, 2017 after it acquired LP Experion. The company raised approximately $3.8, million in 2017.

WeedMD

Ticker: WMD

Exchange: TSXV

Last trade: $1.38

    52 week high: $3.25

    52 week low: $0.68

Shares outstanding: 100.37

Location: Aylmer, ON

Date of initial licensing: April 22, 2016

License type dry: Cultivation and Sale

License type fresh oil: Production and Sale

Size of facility: 26,000 to be 610,000 square feet

Annual production: 1,200 to be 50,000 kgs

Marketing budget: unknown

WMD commenced trading April 27, 2017. The company has announced plans to expand to a 610,000-square-foot facility in Strathroy, Ontario. In September 2017, it announced an agreement with three long-term retirement facilities. In December 2017, a supply agreement was signed with Jarlette Health Services, an Ontario long-term care facility. In March of 2018, WMD applied for a dealer's license with Health Canada and entered a joint venture with Phividia to produce cannabis-infused beverages. Also in March, the company completed a strategic investment in blockchain technology. The company raised approximately $15 million in 2017.

3. The Tool Kit

These are my simplified quick tests to assess investment choices. At this time, I am focusing on shares outstanding, facility sizes, and marketing budgets. As the industry establishes itself, annual reliable production, trade agreements, and earnings per share should also be on the radar. There are many other variables that can offer predictability. My esteemed colleagues may argue that these tests are overly simple.

There is value to in-depth analysis. However, my experience has taught me it is not always possible to do in-depth analysis in venture capital markets. Also, no amount of analysis can predict the human factor.

Warren Buffett has argued the only value with the recent cryptocurrency mania is FOMO: Fear Of Missing Out. I have personally lived through the tech bubble of the 1990s and mining fiasco with Bre-X. No amount of analysis or due diligence could protect investors from those events. So, although in-depth analysis offers value, so do simplified quick tests like these.

3.1 A comparative analysis of LPs' shares outstanding

Market capitalization (CAP) is a popular term, and for me as an experienced investor, it means very little. Market cap is the total market value of the securities of a company. It is calculated by taking the number of issued and outstanding securities, multiplied by the last trading price or closing bid.

A true market cap incorporates more than the shares outstanding. An issuer may have issued securities and then repurchased those securities without cancelling them. In that case, the securities are issued but are not outstanding. As a result, the number of issued securities does not equal the number of outstanding securities. This inflates and dilutes the numbers if you are trying to determine if a company has a low or high trading volume. Another reason I don't use market caps is because two companies can have similar market caps but completely different trading prices or securities outstanding. For example, Company ABC has 1 million shares outstanding and is trading at a price of $5 for a market cap of $5 million. Company XYZ has 5 million shares outstanding with a stock price trading at $1 for the same market cap of $5 million. It can be relevant if trying to assess the market share of an industry. However, this doesn't help while trying to assess if the company is trading higher than normal volumes. For assessing stock prices and trading volumes, I prefer to look at the shares outstanding. I believe it gives a purer reflection of the numbers in the market.

If you are trying to determine the volume of shares trading in a day is low or high, it is helpful to know how many shares are available to trade. The shares outstanding are also a good reflection of the supply and demand rules of economics. The less the supply, the greater the demand. If too many shares are outstanding, the stock price will be diluted and it will take more momentum to see price movements and influxes. If too few shares are outstanding, prices will fluctuate and have rapid volatility. There needs to be a sufficient balance of shares outstanding to accommodate a liquid market.

To simplify, let's compare playing with cards. While playing card games, there is a greater predictability of the possibilities when only one deck is used. When more decks are added to the game, it becomes more difficult to predict what you may get hit with. Same logic applies to shares outstanding. There is a greater predictability of what might happen when there are fewer shares outstanding.

Shares outstanding is also a quick indication for how many times the company has had go to the table to ask for money. When a company raises capital on the stock market, they offer more outstanding shares. It dilutes the stock each time there is a financing. If there are a larger than normal amount of shares outstanding, it can be an indication of poor management. Of course, there are exceptions to this rule. A cannabis company that did a reverse-take-over (RTO) of a mining company may have inherited an exorbitant amount of shares outstanding. However, in general, measuring shares outstanding is a quick, simple test that I have found reliable.

Therefore, I find it preferable to look for companies with fewer shares outstanding. Table 3 is a breakdown of the shares outstanding for the LPs trading on the market.

3.2 A comparative analysis of the LPs' facility size

During this virtual green rush, the goal is to have the greatest market share in the industry (as opposed to the stock market). LPs want to predominantly capture the market with their product. In the years 2016 and 2017, LPs raised hundreds of millions of dollars in an unprecedented economic commitment for an emerging sector. They did this so they could be the first LP with the biggest and best facilities to produce the most product in order to capture the greatest market share. That will impact stock prices. I have made a breakdown of the facility sizes in Table 4.

3.3 A comparative analysis of the LPs' marketing budgets

The biggest threat to the cannabis market is undoing more than 100 years of oppression and stigma. For this reason, I believe the marketing budget is a key factor to an LP's success. I have outlined

Table 3
Shares Outstanding of LPs in Millions as of April 2, 2018

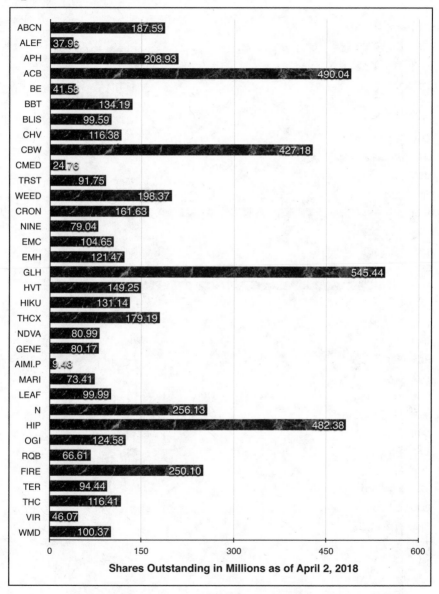

Shares Outstanding in Millions as of April 2, 2018

Ticker	Shares Outstanding (Millions)
ABCN	187.59
ALEF	37.96
APH	208.93
ACB	490.04
BE	41.58
BBT	134.19
BLIS	99.59
CHV	116.38
CBW	427.18
CMED	24.76
TRST	91.75
WEED	198.37
CRON	161.63
NINE	79.04
EMC	104.65
EMH	121.47
GLH	545.44
HVT	149.25
HIKU	131.14
THCX	179.19
NDVA	80.99
GENE	80.17
AIMI.P	9.48
MARI	73.41
LEAF	99.99
N	256.13
HIP	482.38
OGI	124.58
RQB	66.61
FIRE	250.10
TER	94.44
THC	116.41
VIR	46.07
WMD	100.37

Table 4
Known Facility Sizes of LPs in Square Feet as of April 2, 2018

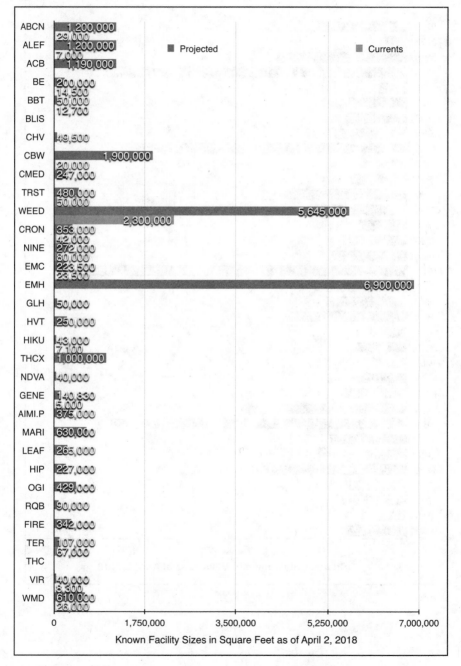

Known Facility Sizes in Square Feet as of April 2, 2018

LP	Projected	Currents
ABCN	1,200,000	29,000
ALEF	1,200,000	7,000
ACB	1,190,000	
BE	200,000	14,500
BBT	50,000	12,700
BLIS		
CHV	49,500	
CBW	1,900,000	20,000
CMED	247,000	
TRST	480,000	50,000
WEED	5,645,000	2,300,000
CRON	353,000	42,000
NINE	272,000	80,000
EMC	223,500	23,500
EMH	6,900,000	
GLH	50,000	
HVT	250,000	
HIKU	43,000	7,100
THCX	1,000,000	
NDVA	40,000	
GENE	140,830	5,000
AIMI.P	375,000	
MARI	630,000	
LEAF	265,000	
HIP	227,000	
OGI	429,000	
RQB	90,000	
FIRE	342,000	
TER	107,000	67,000
THC		
VIR	40,000	8,300
WMD	610,000	26,000

the marketing budgets from the companies that disclosed them in Table 5.

3.4 Licensed Producer applicants

As of May 2017, Health Canada had received more than 1,600 applications for Licensed Producers and more than 400 are being processed. It is highly unlikely all the applicants will be given LP status. There is no way to predict which, when, or how many applicants will be granted LP status.

In December 2016, Parliament was presented with The Canadian Task Force on Cannabis Legalization report. The task force had many mandates including exploring ways cannabis prices could be competitive to curb the illegal market. It suggests if the government can use the granting of LPs as a tool, it can manage the price of cannabis to the end customer. So, if the current number of LPs can't supply the demand for cannabis at competitive prices, the government can grant another applicant LP status. Hence, the race for existing LPs to build more and bigger facilities to curb competitors entering the market. There is a list of LP applicants I have been able to track in Table 6.

4. Ancillary Cannabis Investments

There are several companies other than cannabis growers and LPs which are trading on public markets and are involved with augmenting and contributing to the industry. A Deloitte study released in October of 2016 estimates the markets for products and services such as testing labs, lighting, and security systems could be over twice the market as growers. Deloitte projects a $22 billion annual industry including growers. There are businesses specializing in scientific research, cultivation compliance, lab testing, oil extraction, greenhouse manufacturing and lighting, software security, distribution and delivery, vapourizer manufacturing, pet food production, topical creams and ointments, edibles, beverages, plastics, clothing, and bio fuel. The latest changes to the proposed *Cannabis Act* also made room for micro-cultivation facilities and processing operations to commence. This will no doubt lead to a whole micro industry. Here are investments to watch for, in the next sections.

4.1 Medical research

Although cannabis had been used as a medicine for some millennia, research using modern science on cannabis for medicine is a relatively

Table 5
Known Marketing Budget of LPs for the Year 2017

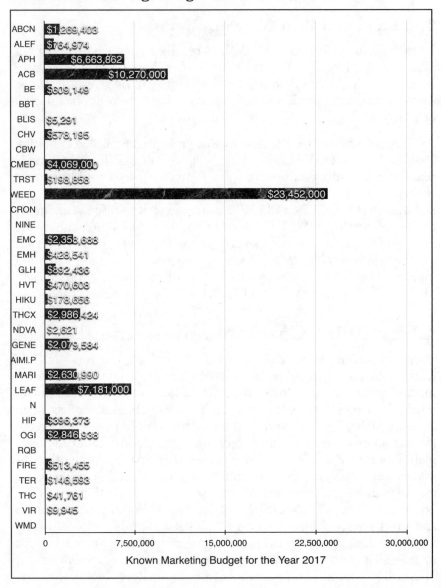

	Known Marketing Budget for the Year 2017
ABCN	$1,269,403
ALEF	$764,974
APH	$6,663,862
ACB	$10,270,000
BE	$609,149
BBT	
BLIS	$5,291
CHV	$578,195
CBW	
CMED	$4,069,000
TRST	$198,858
WEED	$23,452,000
CRON	
NINE	
EMC	$2,358,688
EMH	$428,541
GLH	$892,436
HVT	$470,608
HIKU	$178,656
THCX	$2,986,424
NDVA	$2,621
GENE	$2,079,584
AIMI.P	
MARI	$2,630,990
LEAF	$7,181,000
N	
HIP	$396,373
OGI	$2,846,938
RQB	
FIRE	$513,455
TER	$146,593
THC	$41,761
VIR	$9,945
WMD	

Table 6
Known LP Applicants

Exchange	Snapshot of LP Applicants Trading on Exchanges	Ticker	Shares Outstanding in Millions	Previous Close CDN$ 04/02/2018	52-Week High	52-Week Low	Known Facility Sizes in Square Feet	Notes
CSE	Alliance Growers Corp.	ACG	59.87	0.285	1.39	0.08	11,000	
CSE	Choo Holdings	CHOO	70.02	0.95	1.10	0.13	40,000	
CSE	Heritage Cannabis Holdings	CANN	162.58	0.44	0.05	0.84	15,500 to 38,000 to be 420,000	CGC craft grower
CSE	Liberty Leaf	LIB	107.03	0.40	1.00	0.08		
CSE	Lotus Ventures Inc.	J	57.37	0.38	1.00	0.21	28,000	
TSXV	Maple Leaf Green World	MGW	149.43	0.85	2.06	0.30	80,000	
CSE	Marapharm Ventures	MDM	108.5	0.67	1.38	0.67	22,000	
CSE	Matica Enterprises	MMJ	227.61	0.31	0.81	0.04	10,000	
CSE	Mountain Lake	MLK	37.12	0.05 halt	0.09	0.02	11,000	
CSE	MPX Bioceutical	MPX	355.71	0.70	1.18	0.28	72,342 to be 402,658	
CSE	MYM Nutraceuticals	MYM	108	2.03	5.00	0.18	to be 1,500,000	$10 million Feb. 2018
CSE	New Age Farm	NF	195.82	0.115	0.42	0.05	48,000	
CSE	Puf Ventures	PUF	52.1	0.82	2.09	0.31	8,800 to be 35,000	CGC craft grower
CSE	Sunniva Inc.	SNN	27.09	8.40	17.93	7.40	700,000	CGC craft grower
CSE	True Leaf Medicine	MJ	95.27	0.67	1.90	0.22	25,000 to be 1,000,000	$14 million Jan. 2018
CSE	Valens GroWorks	VGW	72.2	2.10	3.55	0.75	17,000 to be 38,000	CGC craft grower

new field of study. Early clinical studies have verified that cannabis has positive impacts. Definitive clinical studies have proven cannabis minimizes seizures in epileptics. Clinical trials have also verified cannabis will reduce the effects of cancer treatments in children (see Prof. Raphael Mechoulam speak to that at www.youtube.com/watch?v=wYJQreAg3DU). Medicinal cannabis research is making progress with Alzheimer's, Amyotrophic Lateral Sclerosis (also known as ALS, or Lou Gehrig's disease), Multiple Sclerosis, depression, opioid addiction, ocular pressure, pain relief ... and that's just the beginning. This is a new and exciting field and, no doubt, new discoveries will make investors lots of money.

4.2 Product placement

The task force has indicated storefront locations are favourable. This would be on target with Colorado's infrastructure. The task force also points out there is a preexisting infrastructure of storefronts in Canada, considering the existence of dispensaries and compassion clubs. Despite the pre-existence of storefront operations, product placement is in a process of re-creation and development. Each province has the power to choose their product placement distribution system. Most provinces opted to provide online sales via crown corporations. Ontario, Quebec, Nova Scotia, New Brunswick, and Prince Edward Island are creating provincial crown corporations to control distribution and storefronts. The intention is to build models in a similar fashion to their liquor distributors. Manitoba, Saskatchewan, Alberta and Newfoundland have chosen to allow privately owned retail stores. British Columbia has decided to create a private/public hybrid system for retail sales.

4.3 Assurance testing for quality control

This is an emerging field that will create jobs and businesses. New processes will need to be created to teach how to ensure quality control, set up guidelines for uniform and accredited lab testing, and create tools to make the work more efficient.

4.4 Edibles and oil products

Edibles are also an exciting emerging niche within the cannabis industry. In recent modern history, cannabis has been baked in brownies or cake. With new extraction techniques, oils are being used to create a vast variety of food and beverages such as gummy bears, soda pop, and other candy.

A recent product made from cannabis oil is called "shatter." It is a hard-peanut brittle type form of the oil that contains up to 80 percent THC. You don't eat it, but you do vape it. The human body can absorb up to 25 percent THC, so the product is more than what would normally be required. However, it is an indication of the open possibilities created by the oil extracts.

4.5 Paraphernalia

Traditional paraphernalia to consume cannabis such as pipes, rolling papers, and grinders are still used. Vaporizers are a recent tool invented to inhale cannabis buds and oils without combustion. Vaporizers will allow the release of up to 95 percent of the cannabinoids.

4.6 Packaging

Packaging is an emerging industry as the industry requires materials to keep the plant safe from spoiling, minimize odor, and keep the product safe from the hands of the underaged.

4.7 Roadside testing

The *Cannabis Act* accommodates for extra policing powers to assess cannabis impairment. Until a means to measure impairment can be invented, police are authorized to use their instincts and opinions to press charges. This is either incentive to create new specialized equipment, or incentive to become a thriving defense lawyer.

4.8 Marketing and branding

Similar to liquor and tobacco sales in Canada, strict guidelines will be imposed on marketing cannabis. Note, even with the *Cannabis Act*, censorship continues. It will remain illegal to print or publish that cannabis is healthy or to make medical/health claims.

4.9 On-demand delivery

Direct delivery is common business practice in some areas such as Quebec. Cannabis can be delivered easier than a pizza after sending a text. To be competitive with the illicit market, a responsible business standard will have to be developed for direct delivery.

4.10 Education

Informing the public of safe and helpful ways to consume cannabis or educating businesses on how to compete in the market.

4.11 Fertilizers

I'm not a farmer, but I do come from Brandon, Manitoba, which is prime farm country. I thought the science of fertilizers was a well-established industry. However, there are fertilizer companies who specialize in making cannabis better.

4.12 Hemp products

Early Canadian pioneers planted hemp as a barrier between farms to keep the wind from blowing off topsoil. Although hemp does not have any psychoactive effects, it is a relative of the cannabis plant and, therefore, it became a prosecutable offence to grow it during the 1930s. Hemp is being grown again and can be used as a source to create many products. It is said that hemp plastics can be ten times stronger than steel and lighter weight. Plus it is sustainable. Hemp biofuel is another sustainable option to watch for future investments strategies with a social responsibility spin.

See Table 7 for a list of ancillary companies. This is my best effort at time of writing to identify and track ancillary cannabis businesses.

Table 7
Known Ancillary Companies

Exchange	Tracker of Ancillary Companies Trading on Exchanges	Ticker	Shares Outstanding in Millions as of April 2, 2018	Previous Close CDN$ April 2, 2018	52-Week High	52-Week Low	Notes
CSE	Abattis Bioceuticals	ATT	352.53	0.20	0.94	0.06	Is a biotechnology company that invests in the legal cannabis industry.
CSE	Affinor Growers Inc.	AFI	90.21	0.14	0.29	0.06	Vertical farming technology for indoor growth.
CSE	Alternate Health Group	AHG	52.68	1.55	4.10	1.50	Health care research.
CSE	Body and Mind Inc.	BAMM	47.7	0.66	2.09	0.15	Holds license to cultivate and produce marijuana in Nevada.
TSXV	Buzz Capital	BUZ.P	8.2	0.70 halt	0.73	0.12	Acquire Kaya a Jamican integrated cannabis company. Hiku acquired 10% stake in Kaya.
CSE	Cannabix Technologies	BLO	86.46	1.97	3.68	0.51	Developing a breathalyzer for law enforcement and workplace.
CSE	CannaRoyalty	CRZ	46.86	3.90	5.75	1.50	Investing in Intellectual Properties for cannabis companies.
CSE	Cannvas MedTech Inc.	MTEC	0.	0.00	0.00	0.00	Utilizing blockchain Smart Contract technology to secure user.

Table 7 — Continued

Exchange	Tracker of Ancillary Companies Trading on Exchanges	Ticker	Shares Outstanding in Millions as of April 2, 2018	Previous Close CDN$ April 2, 2018	52-Week High	52-Week Low	Notes
CSE	Fincanna Capital Corp.	CALI	66.34	0.62	2.29	0.61	Is a royalty company for licensed medical cannabis, with a special focus on California.
CSE	Friday Night Inc.	TGIF	213.07	0.59	1.48	0.17	Cultivates and produces medical cannabis in the US.
CSE	Global Hemp Group Inc.	GHG	180.73	0.13	0.39	0.02	Acquiring a strategic portfolio of the industrial hemp businesses.
CSE	High Hampton Holdings	HC	26.70	0.98	1.48	0.31	Services LPs, Kelowna.
TSXV	Hempco Food and Fibre	HEMP	49.70	1.53	3.13	0.28	Provides hemp seeds and foods for humans and animals.
TSX	Horizons Medical Marijuana Life Sciences	HMMJ	0.00	16.32	25.56	8.21	Exchange Traded Fund (ETF).
NEO	Horizons Emerging Marijuana Growers Index	HMJR	0.00	8.56	10.45	8.50	Exchange Traded fund (ETF).
CSE	iAnthus	IAN	42.60	3.19	6.39	1.70	Operates American dispensaries in 6 states.
TSXV	International Cannabis Corp.	ICC	137.60	1.30	2.00	0.80	Company is a licensed farm in Uruguay.

Table 7 — Continued

Exchange	Tracker of Ancillary Companies Trading on Exchanges	Ticker	Shares Outstanding in Millions as of April 2, 2018	Previous Close CDN$ April 2, 2018	52-Week High	52-Week Low	Notes
TSX	InMed Pharmaceuticals	IN	152.27	1.36	2.42	0.23	Drug discovery and development.
CSE	Isodiol International Inc.	ISOL	300.78	1.03	2.14	0.10	Develops and markets hemp-based products and solutions in Canada and the US.
TSXV	Kalytera Therapeutics	KALY	132.06	0.34	0.58	0.08	Medical research.
CSE	Liberty Health Sciences	LHS	303.36	0.94	2.88	0.75	Acquiring US-based companies in Florida and Ohio.
CSE	Lifestyle Delivery System	LDS	107.58	0.66	1.54	0.35	Produces smokeless alternative options for cannabis.
CSE	LexariaBio Science Corp.	LXX	71.10	1.24	3.23	0.35	Sells cannabidiol-infused teas.
TSXV	National Access Cannabis Corp.	NAC	130.21	0.93	1.20	0.11	Nationwide chain of cannabis distribution clinics. Won a retail bid in Manitoba.
CSE	Nanosphere Health Sciences	NSHS	96.07	0.55	1.16	0.45	Creation of a platform using nanotechnology for cannabis-health industries.
CSE	Nutritional High International	EAT	270.24	0.41	1.19	0.08	Acquires cannabis and hemp-infused products and brands

Table 7 — Continued

Exchange	Tracker of Ancillary Companies Trading on Exchanges	Ticker	Shares Outstanding in Millions as of April 2, 2018	Previous Close CDN$ April 2, 2018	52-Week High	52-Week Low	Notes
CSE	Phivida Holdings	VIDA	41.64	1.07	2.20	0.62	Produces and sells hemp oil-infused beverages and foods.
CSE	Quadron Cannatech Corp.	QCC	66.45	0.345	0.97	0.19	Provides products and services designed for cannabis in Canada and the US.
TSXV	Radient	RTI	224.08	1.39	2.28	0.41	Is an oil extraction technology company.
TSXV	Revive	RVV	57.52	0.225	0.51	0.13	Acquires, develops, and commercializes medical treatments.
CSE	Wildflower	SUN	44.00	1.52	2.94	0.32	Develops branded cannabis health-care products.
TSX	Village Farms	VFF	42.45	5.13	9.8	1.60	Produces and markets greenhouse products across North America — joint venture with EMH.
CSE	Vodis Pharmaceuticals	VP	30.46	0.315	0.91	0.17	Vaporizing manufacturing company.
CSE	Veritas Pharma	VRT	51.02	0.44	1.09	0.28	Develops medicinal cannabis.

3

Investment Strategies for Cannabis Venture Stocks

The large volume of buyers in the new cannabis industry can be compared to a virtual Gold Rush or in this case, "green rush." When jumping into the venture capital markets, penny stocks can be alluring. It's a lot of fun to buy 5,000 shares at $0.20 for total of a $1,000 investment, and watch the stock go up to $1, to gross $5,000!

Patience is required to buy 1,000 shares at $1.00 with the same $1,000 investment and then wait for the stock to grow to $5.00 (now the stock needs to grow by a dollar four times instead of just once), to gross the same $5,000. It is a harder game. Unfortunately, summer of 2016 was likely the last hurrah to buy any LPs at $0.20.

The cannabis industry does have other potentials for penny stocks that are not LPs. They will be higher risk. To compare with the oil and gas industry, it's like digging a hole because there might be oil below. It requires money or venture capital to dig. We all want to put money in a well that hits oil, but you never know. The well could be a dry hole and a bust. Just like not knowing if the well will strike oil and make millions or be a bust, the same principle applies to the emerging venture cannabis industry. If you buy stock in the right applicant or ancillary company, you may strike it rich. Hence why the higher the risk, the higher the reward.

Buying stock is easy, selling it is hard. Have patience. There are no guarantees. There will be losses. Set goals and sell at those goals. Don't get greedy. Unless you have a magical crystal ball, you will never predict consistently or accurately the highest and lowest trades. The market never goes away so you can always go back in. But ... it's easier said than done when in the back of your mind you are thinking, "I'm going to be rich, the sky is the limit!" It's an exciting feeling. At the end of the day, you are winning if you buy low and sell high.

1. Choosing Your Investments

It cannot be stressed enough, any investment in the cannabis industry will be considered extremely high risk. That is because all cannabis stocks are part of an emerging industry. And stocks in an emerging industry are brand new. Brand new stocks are venture stocks. Venture stocks are extremely high risk. That said, I trust you have made it to this point of the book because you are responsible enough to make your own financial choices and you want to choose the risk. After all, the greater the risk, the greater the reward could be.

This book provides several possibilities to choose for cannabis investments. Assess your budget and choose a stock that will fit in that budget, and go with your instinct. You might prefer to choose a stock that is associated with where you live. You may want to stick to investing in LPs. Or, you might be more keen on the emerging edible or medical research stocks. Whatever your interests, the ultimate choice of which stocks to buy is yours. I have developed a decision-making matrix to help assess investment choices.

1.1 Decision-making matrix

A decision-making matrix can help compare companies' strengths and weaknesses and assess competitive advantages. In my current matrix, I consider the size of the facilities, the amount of shares outstanding, the marketing budget, and the price range of the stock. A subjective grade between 1-10 has been given depending on how successful the companies are with each factor; 1 means "not great; room for improvement" and 10 means they are doing a "good" job. The picture it forms will help assess which companies will be a worthy investment to own. Table 8 demonstrates my assessment of cannabis investments at the time of writing. Readers should do their own due diligence and research to verify their numbers before they invest.

Table 9 shows my decision-making matrix for applicants.

2. Diversifying Investments

If you are investing with a budget of $1,000 or less, I suggest focusing on one company. However, when possible, diversifying is always recommended. It is the simple economic theory of not putting all your eggs in one basket.

3. Time Frame for Investments

The suggested goal is to have as many cannabis shares as possible before it is legalized for recreational purposes. The Trudeau party introduced and passed the first reading of a bill that legalized cannabis in April 2017. The house passed the third reading of the bill November 27, 2017, and sent it to senate. Senate commenced reading the bill in February 2018, and had passed the second reading by late March. The suggested goal is to have recreational cannabis available in stores by summer of 2018.

According to investment regulators, any investment under three years is considered a short-term investment. Venture capital investments by their nature are expected to be short-term investments. Waves will be created in the markets once cannabis is legalized. I expect to see skyrocketing peaks as announcements are made for legalization time frames.

This could be followed by volatile crashes. This is because cannabis stocks are currently trading on projections. They are trading at elevated values based on future sales. Stock markets have, dare I say, volatile emotions. Investors will buy on rumour, but sell on the facts. They will buy stock that is overvalued based on future profits, but sell when they realize it will take time to achieve those profits. Stocks will rise and fall back with no change in the company's actual current value.

This creates choices for investment strategy time frames. You may choose to buy stock for a quick flip. Or you may choose to buy and hold as the industry continues to emerge. The strategy is up to you. I prefer a buy and hold strategy. When I see an anomaly in the market, I will sell a portion of my holdings if the stock seems high.

Table 8
Decision-Making Matrix for Licensed Producers as of April 2, 2018

	Key Factors	Size of Facility	Price Range of Stock	Shares Outstanding	Marketing Budget	Total Weight
Licensed Producers	**Weight**	**35**	**30**	**25**	**10**	**100**
ABCann Global	ABCN	10 350	9 270	3 75	2 20	**715**
Aleafia Health Inc.	ALEF	10 350	10 300	9 225	1 10	**885**
Aphria	APH	10 350	1 30	2 50	10 100	**530**
Aurora Cannabis Inc.	ACB	10 350	2 60	1 25	10 100	**535**
Beleave Kannabis	BE	2 70	8 240	9 225	1 10	**545**
Benchmark Botanics	BBT	0.5 17.5	9 270	5 125	0 0	**413**
Bliss Co Holdings Ltd.	BLIS	0 0	10 300	6 150	1 10	**460**
Canada House Wellness	CHV	0.495 17.325	10 300	6 150	1 10	**477**
Cannabis Wheaton	CBW	10 350	8 240	1 25	0 0	**615**
CanniMed Ltd.	CMED	2.47 86.45	1 30	10 250	8 80	**446**

Table 8 — Continued

CannTrust Inc.	TRST	4.8	3	7	1	
		168	90	175	10	**443**
Canopy Growth	WEED	10	1	3	10	
		350	30	75	100	**555**
Cronos Group	CRON	3.53	2	4	0	
		123.55	60	100	0	**284**
Delta 9	NINE	2.72	9	7	0	
		95.2	270	175	0	**540**
Emblem	EMC	2.235	9	6	4	
		78.225	270	150	40	**538**
Emerald Health Therapeutics	EMH	10	6	6	1	
		350	180	150	10	**690**
Golden Leaf Holdings	GLH	0.5	10	1	1	
		17.5	300	25	10	**353**
Harvest One	HVT	2.5	10	5	1	
		87.5	300	125	10	**523**
Hiku	HIKU	0.43	8	5	1	
		15.05	240	125	10	**390**
Hydro-pothecary	THCX	10	7	3	6	
		350	210	75	60	**695**
Indiva	NDVA	0.4	10	7	1	
		14	300	175	10	**499**
Invictus MD Strategies	GENE	1.4	9	7	4	
		49	270	175	40	**534**
AIM1 Ventures	AIMI.P	3.75	10	10	0	
		131.25	300	250	0	**681**
MariCann Inc.	MARI	6.3	9	8	5	
		220.5	270	200	50	**741**

Table 8 — Continued

MedReleaf Corp.	LEAF	2.65 92.75	1 30	6 150	10 100	**373**
Namaste Technolo-gies	N	0 0	9 270	1 25	0 0	**295**
Newstrike Resources	HIP	2.27 79.45	9 270	1 25	1 10	**384**
Organigram	OGI	4.29 150.15	7 210	5 125	5 50	**535**
Ravenquest BioMed	RQB	0.9 31.5	9 270	8 200	0 0	**502**
The Supreme Cannabis Company	FIRE	3.42 119.7	9 270	1 25	1 10	**425**
Terrascend Corp.	TER	1.07 37.45	6 180	7 175	1 10	**402**
THC Biomed Intl Ltd.	THC	0 0	9 270	6 150	1 10	**430**
Viridium Pacific Group	VIR	0.4 14	9 270	9 225	0 0	**509**
WeedMD Inc.	WMD	6.1 213.5	9 270	6 150	0 0	**634**

Table 9
Decision-Making Matrix for Applicants
as of April 2, 2018

	Key Factors	Size of facility	Price range of stock	Shares outstanding	Total weight
LP Applicants	Weight	35	35	30	100
Alliance Growers Corp.	ACG	0.11 3.85	10 350	8 240	**594**
Choo Holdings	CHOO	0.4 14	9 315	8 240	**569**
Heritage Cannabis Holdings	CANN	4.2 147	10 350	4 120	**617**
Liberty Leaf	LIB	0 0	9 315	6 180	**495**
Lotus Ventures Inc.	J	0.28 9.8	10 350	8 240	**600**
Maple Leaf Green World	MGW	0.8 28	9 315	4 120	**463**
Marapharm Ventures	MDM	0.22 7.7	9 315	6 180	**503**
Matica Enterprises	MMJ	0.1 3.5	10 350	2 60	**414**
Mountain Lake	MLK	0.11 3.85	10 350	9 270	**624**
MPX Bioceutical	MPX	4.03 141.05	9 315	1 30	**486**
MYM Nutraceuticals	MYM	10 350	6 210	6 180	**740**

Table 9 — Continued

New Age Farm	NF	0.48	10	3	
		16.8	350	90	**457**
Puf Ventures	PUF	0.35	9	8	
		12.25	315	240	**567**
Sunniva Inc.	SNN	7	1	9	
		245	35	270	**550**
True Leaf Medicine	MJ	10	9	7	
		350	315	210	**875**
Valens GroWorks	VGW	0.38	6	8	
		13.3	210	240	**463**

I'm usually lucky to buy back at a lower price. The risk is the stock might continue to rise, which does happen, so I end up buying back fewer shares at higher prices. But the odds are the stocks will drop after a big rally. After doing this a few times, I will end up with excess cash. With that, I buy stocks when I see a low anomaly. Sometimes it works out that I can average out a lower cost of shares I already own. But for my overall portfolio, my strategy is buy and hold, and patience.

Once cannabis is legalized, and I firmly believe it will become legalized, I predict short-term volatile up and down swings and waves. However, as the industry emerges it is not unreasonable to expect a decade-long bull market.

3.1 Reasons to buy before cannabis is legalized

There is the risk that cannabis will not be legalized for recreational purposes. The senate could offer resistance to the bill. This will not affect the current medicinal cannabis market that has already been legalized and is authorized under the *Canada Health Act*. Cannabis LP stock prices will decline but it is highly unlikely that operations will cease altogether if legalization does not happen. Although all cannabis stocks are high risk, there is less risk of losing all your investment with an LP.

Canadian LPs raised an estimated $1.2 billion for the cannabis industry in the first six weeks of 2018 which is more than double the amount raised in 2017. In the United States, where cannabis remains federally illegal, there are limited channels for money to be raised.

In January of 2018, Bank of Montreal was the first of Canada's big six banks to enter the market prior to full legalization when it invested $175 million in Canopy Growth. In February of 2018, Sun Life Assurance Co. became the first major insurance company to add cannabis to its group benefit plans. Mutual funds and pension funds with low risk tolerance mandates are not yet buying into the cannabis market. Because of low risk tolerance mandates, they must wait until cannabis is fully legalized before they can invest. Stock prices will increase as more insurance policies, mutual funds, pension funds, and banks begin to invest in cannabis.

Canada has set the stage as the first G7 nation to legalize cannabis, and other countries are watching as we create the standards. Many countries have started to legalize medicinal cannabis. However, they are looking at deals with Canadian LPs to provide the product. This is because Canadian LPs are establishing guidelines for safe product. Many of the LPs have locked in distribution deals with countries in Europe, Australia, and South America.

4
Investing in the Stock Market 101

If you are like me and were about to go on a trip to a casino you might need to brush up on a few things. I would focus on one game, such as blackjack. If it were me, I would need to relearn some rules and the value of the chips.

I think most people feel that way about jumping in the stock market. All they need to do is learn a few rules and values. When I was a discount broker, I realized it wasn't just the rules people didn't understand, it was the language. Imagine what it would be like if you were going to a casino, but didn't know what a deck of cards was?

Take a step back here and think about a deck of cards. Do you remember learning the difference between a low card and a face card or if an ace is high or low? How many cards are there in a deck? Do you count them by suit or by number? This may seem simple and childish to you now. Knowing how to read a deck of cards is the first fundamental understanding of casino games. The deck is a language unto itself. If you have never seen a deck of cards, a casino and all its games would be overwhelming.

When learning to invest in the stock market, you first need to understand the basic language. Learning a new language can feel overwhelming. So, forgive me for taking this down to an elementary level, but it is probably the level you would have been at when you first learned to read a deck of cards.

So, with that said, let's start learning how to play in the stock markets!

1. Opening a Brokerage Account

Let's begin with opening an account. I recommend doing this first because sometimes it will take a few days or weeks to sort out the account administration. Think of it as booking your hotel room for Vegas. While the account administration is sorting out, you can prepare yourself by monitoring and choosing your investments.

Each of the big six Canadian banks has discount brokerages attached to them. Each brokerage firm has pros and cons and none is perfect. You may find it easiest to open an account with the brokerage attached to your bank. It does make things simpler for moving money back and forth, but it is not always the best choice. You may find another brokerage house can accommodate you better than your own bank. Here is a breakdown of the big six discount brokerages plus two national independents (prices were current at time of writing):

- CIBC Investor Edge $6.95/trade

- Bank of Montreal Investor Line $9.95/online trade

- National Bank Direct Brokerage 9.95/trade

- RBC Direct Investing $9.95/trade

- Scotia iTrade $24.99/trade

- TD Direct Investing $9.99/trade

- Qtrade Investor $8.75/trade

- Quest Trade $9.95/trade

The highest commissioned discount brokerage house is Scotia iTrade. It can be noted its commission base drops if you have its minimum account level ($50,000). Some of the brokerages have a variable commission fee less than that listed above if you reach their minimum account level or due to a minimum amount of trades.

For any of the firms listed, you can download forms and follow their instructions to mail or fax them in for processing. Alternatively, you may go into any of the banks and ask for assistance to open an account with their associated discount brokerage house. Note that, although the banks own the firms, bankers have not been trained on investment industry regulations for brokerages. They can assist you with the forms, but they very likely do not know the forms any better than you do. If you feel you need assistance with the forms, call the toll-free phone number for the brokerage house you choose. They are more trained and capable than bankers to meet your stock brokerage administration needs.

1.1 Types of brokerage accounts

If you have contribution room, a tax-free savings account (TFSA) is an excellent vehicle to use to invest in stocks. I will never stop getting giddy saying I'm making money on cannabis legally and it's tax free!

A Registered Retirement Savings Plan (RRSP) would also work, if you prefer. If you don't have contribution room for a tax-free investment, you can also buy stocks in a cash account. This is a simple, straightforward account. More sophisticated investors also have the option of using margin, options, or short accounts. That is beyond the scope of this book.

2. How Much Money Do You Need?

Your budget must be determined by your own comfort level. Ask yourself directly, "How much can I afford to lose?" Losing the entire investment is a worst-case scenario. If using a tax avoidance account (TFSA or RRSP), you cannot lose more than the original investment. The same is true for a cash account. A more sophisticated investor with a margin or short account could lose more money, but that's for another book. I suggest an approximate minimum of $1,000 to begin. Then tell yourself directly, "I'm going to win!"

3. A Little Lingo for Stock Market Newbies

As a discount stockbroker, I used to keep a list on my desk of the most popular questions clients would ask. The next sections lists the most popular answers.

3.1 What is a stock anyway?

A stock represents ownership. Buying a stock means buying a piece of a company. It is like owning a very small piece of a much bigger pie. The word originated from trading stocks of hay. Other terms used for stocks are "equity" or "shares." A stock is also called a "security."

A security is an investment contract that is transferable. A stock is a security. Other examples of securities are bonds, mutual funds, and derivatives such as rights, warrants, call and put options.

3.2 Ticker symbol

A ticker symbol is a short, abbreviated name representing a company on the stock exchange. It is typically three or four letters. Hopefully they make sense and somewhat resemble the stock name, but that is not a rule. For example, THC Biomed has been fortunate with the stock ticker symbol THC. However, with mergers and acquisitions and name changes, the ticker symbol does not always reflect the company name. Canopy Growth which began as Tweed, has changed its ticker from TWD to CGC to WEED.

3.3 Bid

To bid means to buy!

3.4 Ask or offer

An ask or an offer means to sell. Note, the term "offer" means the exact opposite in the real estate industry where it means to buy. In the investment world, an offer means to sell!

3.5 Board lots

Board lots are stocks that trade in bundles. In the Vegas analogy, the board lots can be compared to poker chips.

It is desirable to buy an even board lot. Anything less than a board lot is called an odd lot. Odd lots are like a broken poker chip. They are undesirable because a premium charge can be applied at the house traders' discretion. The traders are confined by a maximum premium charge but they usually have the discretion to add a penny or two to the price of an odd lot trade. Therefore, customers have less control setting a trading price for odd lots. It can work to the customers' advantage but it seldom goes that way. It is important to know what the board lots are while calculating how many shares you are going to purchase and at what price.

There are different sized board lots for different price ranges. The different sizes could be compared to the assorted colours and therefore different values of the poker chips.

- Anything below a dime needs 1,000 shares for a board lot

- $.010–$0.99 needs 500 shares for a board lot

- •$1.00 and over needs 100 shares for a board lot

3.6 Limit price

A limit price allows you to choose the price you want to buy or sell your stock. Venture markets can be volatile, so I like to set limits.

3.7 Market order

A market order is an order to submit your buy or sell order at the next available price. The advantage is the order will be guaranteed a fill immediately. It can be used in a fast market to complete a trade quickly. The risk is if there is a temporary gap in the market, it is possible to buy or sell at an unpredictable price that could be unfavourable.

3.8 Day trade

A day trade is a choice to enter a trade for a day or longer. A day trade order will be automatically cancelled or "killed" at the end of the day if it was not filled. I like day trades because it forces me to monitor the markets daily for anomalies. Markets can change with news overnight, so a day trade allows a fresh start each day. In the movies, the little pieces of paper thrown in the air are day trades that were not filled and so killed at the end of the day. Paper tickets no longer exist due to computer technology, so this doesn't normally happen anymore.

3.9 Open or good 'til cancelled order

An open, or good 'til cancelled order is the opposite of a day trade. It allows a limit order to remain active for a preset number of days. This can be helpful if it is not possible to monitor the markets for a period. For example, you may have a work conflict or be planning a holiday. The TSX allows open orders for a maximum of 90 days. However, most brokerages will cap off an open order at 30 days. The risk is getting the order filled at an undesirable price if there has been a material change or news release while not watching the markets.

3.10 Settlement periods

Trading a stock is entering a contract with preset terms for payment, delivery, and time frames. Canada recently made changes to its settlement periods. Commencing September 5, 2017, settlement periods decreased to two days. That means the buyer must pay for a purchase or the seller must deliver the securities sold on or before the second business day after the transaction. For example, if a stock trades on a Friday, it will settle the following Tuesday with the following exceptions:

- RRSPs and TFSAs require funds be in the account before a trade is allowed, so the settlement period isn't as relevant for buy orders. However, if selling in an RRSP or TFSA, it is required to wait a two-day settlement period before it's possible to deregister and remove funds.

- In cash accounts the funds are required within two business days' time frame for a buy order. The exception may be if a firm requires cash up front for a first-time trade. The settlement period to remove funds for sell orders in a cash account is the same two-business-day wait as an RRSP or TFSA.

Note: If selling a stock in any account, the funds are available the same day to purchase another stock in the same account. For example, if stock in company XYZ sells on a Monday, the funds in the account are available that same Monday to buy shares in company ABC. It's only a requirement to wait two business days to remove the funds from the account.

3.11 At the market

At the market means the last trading price or bid of the current active market of a stock. If a stock last traded at $2.50, the "at-the-market" price is $2.50. If you are selling the stock and the bid is $2.50 and you decide to "hit the bid," you are selling "at the market." If the offer is at $2.50 and you are buying a stock at $2.50, you are buying "at the market." It basically means the "price right now."

3.12 Special handling

Special handling refers to orders that must trade under special conditions. They are seldom used in venture capital markets.

3.13 All or none (AON)

All or none (AON) is a special term order where the quantity must be filled completely or the trade will not take place. It can be put on a trade where an odd lot is involved, but the house traders can still trade around them or place a premium on the odd lot if they choose. There are not a lot of practical uses for this option, but some people like it.

3.14 On-stop (OS) order

An on-stop (OS) is a special term order. It is an open order that is triggered by a stop price. There are OS buy orders and OS sell orders. They must be either a limit or market order. It is designed as an "insurance type" tool to minimize your risk of loss. OS market orders are risky for the same reason as a market order. If there is a temporary gap in the market you can be filled at an unfavourable price. This is considered riskier since it could be triggered at a future time while you are not monitoring the market. It could also minimize your potential for profits. If you are okay with making some money and walking away from a potential jackpot, then this tool is for you. However, that's not usually the purpose of venture capital. I have worked with hundreds of brokers and traders at a handful of venture capital firms and I have experienced only one broker who uses the OS tool. He does use it successfully in venture capital fast markets. His clients accept they are making minimal gains, but are also making minimal losses. On average, they are winning over a long period of time. Venture capital by nature is virtually always considered short term, high reward investments. However, using the OS tool over the long term is something to be considered.

3.15 Market capitalization

Market capitalization (market cap) is the total market value of the securities of a company. It is calculated by taking the number of issued and outstanding securities, multiplied by the last trading price or closing bid. Outstanding securities are the stocks for a company trading on the market, termed "shares outstanding."

3.16 Halt trading

Halt trading is a temporary stoppage of trading of the stock which may be imposed by the exchange, its agent, or by voluntary request of the company. If a company requests its stock to be halted, it is typically to make an announcement. If the exchange or agent requests a halt, it is because it has found an indication of non-compliance of regulations. The stock is halted so the public can have a fair and equal opportunity to review the news before stock trades commence.

4. How to Read a Stock Quote

The previous section outlined the components to a stock quote. A standard stock quote will read in the following order:

1. The ticker symbol, which is the three- to four-letter abbreviation representing the stock.

2. The last trade price.

3. The change up or down from the previous trade. Can be expressed in dollar value or percentage.

4. The current bid of the stock, with the current number of board lots on the bid. **Note:** It's normally board lots that are displayed on the bid and asks, not the number of shares. Also, the board lots are usually smaller font or are separated in brackets to distinguish the number from the bid price.

5. The current ask of the stock with the number of board lots on the ask. The board lots are usually displayed with smaller font or in brackets so they can be distinguished from the offer.

6. The volume of shares traded that day. **Note:** This number expresses shares, not board lots.

7. The day high and low trading price.

8. Last is usually the 52-week high and low prices. See Example 1.

Example 1
Stock Quote

Ticker	Last Price	Change	Bid (size)	Ask (size)	Volume	Day High	Day Low	52-Week High	52-Week Low
ABC	$10.50	-0.1	$10.00 (100)	$11.00 (150)	1,535,000	$12.00	$10.00	$14.50	$5.25

> The ticker symbol is? _____
>
> How many board lots are on the bid? _____
>
> How many shares are on the offer? _____
>
> What was the day low? _____
>
> What was the 52-week high? _____
>
> What was the last trade of the day? _____
>
> What is the trading volume? _____
>
> What is the bid price? _____

5. Canadian Stock Exchanges

Stock exchanges originated in the middle ages in London, England. Coffee shops served as meeting places for brokers to buy and sell farm crops and livestock. Trading opportunities increased with the discovery of the Americas and East India route. The capital pools massed too large for single brokers to trade which gave motivation to create the London, New York, Montreal, and Toronto stock exchanges. Today they are used to trade virtually any commodity, service, or business imaginable.

The purpose of stock exchanges is to provide a liquid market to trade securities. They offer a market center for frequent sales, a narrow price spread, and small price fluctuations for trades. Credible exchanges offer personal trust, transparent disclosure, and regulation of members.

For our purposes, there are three Canadian stock exchanges to note. The Toronto Stock Exchange (TSX), the Venture Exchange (TSXV) and the Canadian Securities Exchange (CSE). All three exchanges are administered for timely disclosure requirements by the Investment Industry Regulatory Organization of Canada (IIROC). IIROC is the Canadian investment industry's self-regulatory organization that oversees all brokers and their brokerage houses and any trading activity of stocks and bonds on all Canadian stock exchanges. Its mandate is to "enforce high quality regulatory and investment standards to protect investors and strengthen market integrity while maintaining efficient and competitive capital markets." The services of IIROC give all three exchanges credibility.

5.1 Toronto Stock Exchange (TSX)

The TSX is considered the most credible Canadian exchange. It was founded in 1852 and incorporated in 1878. Because it has existed for more than a century it has an established record which offers credibility for investors' confidence. The downside is that it is also the most expensive stock exchange on which to list a company. This is a consideration when you are buying a startup company that needs to mitigate costs. As cannabis is an emerging industry all its companies are startups.

5.2 TSX Venture Exchange (TSXV)

The TSXV is an amalgamation of the Alberta Stock Exchange and the Vancouver Stock Exchange which occurred in 1999. They merged to make the exchanges more uniform and transparent for international identity. Two years after this merge, the exchange moved east to Toronto. It is now considered the "little board" for the TSX. Although listing costs are lower than the TSX, more regulatory and administration fees became applicable to the TSXV because of working directly under the "big board."

5.3 Canadian Securities Exchange (CSE)

After the TSXV moved to Toronto, a fair market for venture seed capital was difficult to establish for small to medium enterprises. The Canadian Securities Exchange was born in 2003 to fill the gap. It is based in Toronto and Vancouver and it operates in a similar fashion to the way the TSXV did before moving to Toronto. There are less regulation requirements and, therefore, far fewer fees. This is extremely attractive for companies trying to save costs while starting up. Although new, and, therefore, considered high risk, the CSE quickly established credibility for venture capital markets. It gained much notoriety and positive public exposure for taking public Canada's first cannabis company Tweed. Tweed is now known as Canopy Growth (WEED), which has since graduated to the "big board" on the TSX.

6. How to Place a Trade

Every trading platform can be a wee different, but they all cover the same fundamentals based on this list:

1. Account

2. Buy or a sell

3. Ticker symbol

4. Market

5. Quantity of shares

6. Order price (limit, market, or stop)

7. Order expiry or term

8. Special handling (all or none option, or early settlement)

9. Payment

10. Commissions

Discount brokerages offer the choice of placing the trades independently online or by phoning into a live broker for assistance. Firms may charge a premium for the phone-in service. The phone-in service will offer guidance and comfort if you are nervous about trading on your own. Either service requires the exact same information. Below are the steps to walk through.

6.1 How to place a bid

1. Select your account. Be sure you are in the correct account.

2. What is the trading action you are about to do: a buy or a sell? If it's your first trade, the answer is buy.

3. The ticker symbol of the company.

4. The market. The online trading platforms for the discount houses will ask if you want to place the trade in the Canadian or American markets. The stocks in this book focus on Canadian stocks trading on Canadian exchanges. There are additional costs and foreign exchange rates charged by trading Canadian stocks on US exchanges. Additionally, it can be tricky to own an American stock in a Canadian tax-avoidance portfolio such as an RRSP or TFSA. I suggest choosing Canadian. The online trading platform will automatically select the Canadian stock exchange (TSX, TSXV, CSE) that has the best price for your trade.

5. Quantity of shares. To choose the number of shares, first consider the board lots. If in Vegas, it would be the same as trying

to determine which poker chips you are playing and how many chips you can afford to play. To calculate the amount of board lots possible to trade, first look at the last trading price or closing bid of the stock. (Board lots below a dime are 1,000, between a dime and $0.99 are 500 and anything above one dollar trades at even increments of 100.) Assess your budget and the amount of board lots you can afford. Now just to make it confusing, when entering the order, you have to enter the number of shares, not the number of board lots!

For example: You have $1,200 to invest. You have found company XYZ whose stocks you want to buy and which is trading at $0.95. You believe that is a fair price. Since the stock is trading above a dime and below $1, the board lots are 500 shares. With a budget of $1,200, you can buy two board lots which equals 1,000 shares (2 x 500 = 1000). The price of your stock will be 1000 shares multiplied by the price of $0.95 (1000 x $0.95 = $950 without commission).

If the same XYZ stock is trading above $1 the board lots change to 100 shares. With the same scenario of a budget of $1,200 and a stock price of $1.05 you can buy 11 board lots (11 x 100 = 1,100) which is 1,100 shares. The stock purchase price will be 1,100 shares multiplied by the price $1.05 (1,100 x $1.05 = $1,155 without commission).

6. Order price. The choice will be to enter a limit price or a market order. I like choosing a limit price. This means I choose the price at which I will buy the stock. The cannabis industry is an emerging market. Emerging markets are volatile. Prices can swing up and down very rapidly. By setting a limit price, I will not be hit with a surprise when I get the bill.

The alternative to a limit order is placing a market order. A market order means the order will be filled at the next available price. If there is a gap in the market, it's possible the order will get filled at an undesirable price.

Choosing your price depends on your budget, comfort level, and how fast the markets are moving. There are pros and cons and risk no matter what price you choose. I like to look at the day high and low and the volume for trades. I pick a price that is either "at the market" or a few cents below. After placing a bid, patience is key. This can be exciting and there is the risk the trade won't be filled.

If the stock price is moving rapidly and it's too big a risk to lose the opportunity, the order can be placed at the ask price or a few cents above. Whatever the choice, I can promise this: It is not possible to consistently choose the highest or lowest price of the day. Once the choice is made, it is a leap of faith, chance, and hope.

7. Order expiry or term. An order can be placed for a day or longer. I like to use day orders. A day order expires at the end of the day. If there is a news announcement overnight, there is an opportunity to assess the situation before reentering the market in the morning.

8. Special handling orders. These are difficult to manage in fast markets, and traders can navigate around them. I recommend not using this tool for the purposes of trading venture stock.

9. Payment. If trading in a TFSA or RRSP, cash needs to be in the account up front before executing a buy order. If trading in a cash account, there is a two-day settlement period before payment is obliged. Firms are within their rights to request the cash up front, especially if it is the first trade.

    Brokerage platforms vary with their operations for accommodating payments and electronic funds transfers. Brokerage firms cannot accept direct payment from a leveraged product such as a credit card.

10. Commission. Brokerage firms charge a fee for using their services. They will automatically calculate it into the cost of the trade. Be sure to calculate for the commission while assessing the cost of buying the stock and budget.

6.2 How to change an order

The online trading platforms will assist through a change order. Typically, go to the order entry page to review the order. Simply click on the order to change and follow the prompts. It is possible to change the price or the volume of shares after submitting if the order has not been filled. Depending on the trading platform, sometimes they will only allow changes with the price and not the number of shares or vice versa. That is a limitation in the trading platform programming. Sometimes it is easier to cancel the order and resubmit.

Exercise 2
Buying Shares

> You have $3,000 and are interested in buying some shares of company ABC which is currently trading at $2.30/ share with a brokerage commission of $6.95/trade.
>
> How many shares can you buy? _____
>
> How many board lots can you buy? _____
>
> How much will the trade cost with commission? _____
>
> How long will be the term of the order? _____
>
> Read the order out loud _____
>
> I'm going to buy _____ shares at a price of $2.30/ share for the term of one day in Canadian dollars.

6.3 How to cancel an order

An order can be canceled if it has not been filled. While reviewing the order, click on the order and follow the prompts to cancel.

6.4 How to place a sell or offer

1. Open the account. Be sure it is the correct account.

2. Select "Sell" as the trade action.

3. Enter the ticker symbol of the company. The brokerage house trading platform may provide a drop-down box with a selection of the stocks owned in your portfolio. This is a handy feature. Be sure to choose the correct ticker symbol.

4. The market. If you have bought your stocks in the Canadian market, then choose Canadian market again to sell your stocks.

5. Quantity of shares. Board lots still apply. Unless the stock has gone through a material change such as a merger, consolidation, or stock split, you should still own even board lots. You can choose to sell all your position or just a portion.

6. Order price. For the reasons under how to buy a stock, I still recommend choosing a Limit price.

7. Order expiry or term. Same as buy orders, I like to use day orders.

8. Special handling. Again, same as a buy order, I recommend not using this tool.

9. Payment. You can choose to leave the funds in the account or move them out. If you choose to leave the funds in the account, you may use those funds to proceed buying another stock the same day. If moving funds out of the account, you must wait two business days before the trade contract will settle and funds are freed to be removed.

10. Commission will be automatically subtracted from the proceeds.

7. How to Read a Stock Chart

Stockbrokers are trained to read charts to help indicate the future direction of a stock price. A scientist would have issues trying to verify if there is any true validity in using charts. I liken it to a crystal ball. Having said that, they are used. A popular tool is the shoulder-head-shoulder historical price chart. The picture will depict the human body with two shoulders and a head. Table 10 is a one-month trading chart for Cronos Group in March 2017. Can you see the heads and the shoulders? Can you determine where the stock price will be going next? Do you see the magic?

Table 10
Head and Shoulder Stock Chart

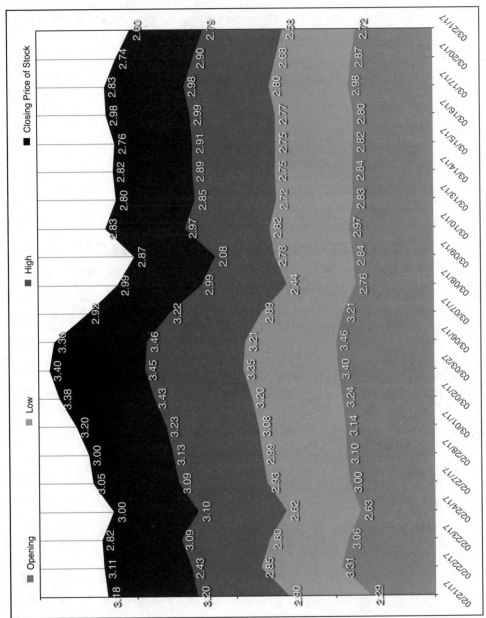

5
Changing Cannabis Credibility

While preparing to write this book, I conducted an informal multiple-choice survey on all my social media sites posing the question: "The biggest challenge to the emerging cannabis industry is undoing over 100 years of ... ?"

- censorship

- fear

- ignorance

- oppression

- persecution

- prejudice

- prohibition

- social shaming

- stigma

- suppression

I confess that ten options are twice the recommendation for a multiple-choice survey. However, I did feel all these terms were relevant.

The survey verified that oppression and stigma are the two biggest challenges. What I found more revealing is that only 1 out of 20 people who opened the survey had actually provided answers. Over 80 people opened the survey, but only 4 responded. Although the terms fear and ignorance were never selected, it would seem logical to conclude those, too, are overwhelming factors.

Deliberate misdirection of facts and extreme suppression of information has pressured society to believe an enormously misguided idea. Dr. Donald Abrams is a doctor who was on the front lines treating AIDS during the crisis in the 1980s. He is now the Chief of Hematology-Oncology at San Francisco General Hospital. For decades, he has done substantial clinical research using cannabis to treat the sick. His research suggests cannabis works better than many synthetic drugs. He would have to prescribe several synthetic drugs, which are more toxic with greater side effects, to do what cannabis does. He says, "it is unfortunately all about politics and not about science." He also points out, cannabis has been used on the planet for medicinal purposes longer than it hasn't been used. To put in perspective, it was used for several thousand years, but has barely been used for the past 100 years. Science, medicine, and history all verify that cannabis is helpful. But for the past century, in many places, it has been a criminal offence to write or publish anything advocating or promoting use of cannabis. It is noteworthy, the new proposed *Cannabis Act* of 2017 has mandated that cannabis cannot be described as "healthy." So, it's understandable that people are still scared and confused. Extreme censorship has been a controlling force in fear and ignorance. This has been a familiar story in history.

To look at Earth's history, there is the obvious comparison of the unjustified persecution of Galileo with his "crazy" theory the Earth revolves around the sun. Galileo was found guilty of heresy and spent the final years of his life under house arrest. Despite his fate, perseverance of the facts and education eventually made it acceptable for society to believe the sun was the center of the solar system and not planet Earth.

A similar story with food for thought is that of the tomato.

The tomato has a volatile history. There is a long-standing joke about the controversies surrounding the tomato. For example, do you say tomāto or tomăto? But the more serious controversy is if a tomato is a fruit or vegetable? Science says it's a fruit. However, at the turn of the last century, the supreme court of the United States ruled it a vegetable so a higher tax could be imposed. Despite the facts, that illogical American law still stands today. This isn't the only time the tomato has found itself in controversy in Earth's history. Tomatoes were once illegal in England and were prohibited in the rest of Europe. It was a crime to grow, distribute, sell, or buy tomatoes. They were believed to be deadly and termed "the poisonous apple." Seems mind boggling, doesn't it? In England, a typical meal was a stew prepared in a clay pot that remained heated over a fire. When you caught a rabbit or picked some vegetables, you threw it in the existing stew. This way the stew could be stretched out for days. When tomatoes were added to the stew, people got sick and died, hence tomatoes were outlawed in England for more than a century.

Science eventually revealed it wasn't the tomato that was killing people but what they were doing with it. Tomatoes will leach acid, causing hairline splits in the pot. Over time, bacteria would build in the cracks causing illness and death. Once metal pots were introduced, the problem could be resolved, but it took time for science to expose the facts.

A similar problem was happening in France where a fad developed to eat on pewter plates. The acid leached from the tomatoes on the pewter, which caused lead poisoning and death. The oppression against the tomato in Europe lasted more than 200 years. They found acceptance in the late 1880s in Italy, when tomatoes were reintroduced as a food that could be cooked on a bread called pizza. Ironically it was about the same time the cannabis persecution began. The economics of the tomato emerged so fast, the US had to figure out how to make money on them, hence the strange unjust law. Despite the controversy, unless you are at La Tomatina festival in Spain where they are tossed at tourists, the tomato is considered safe and acceptable these days. Two hundred years of tomato oppression was changed because of a new message they were safe and healthy and because pizza is awesome.

In an ironic twist of fate, a recent change with the tomato industry has created an opportunity for the cannabis industry. Until recently, the town of Leamington, Ontario was considered the Tomato Capital of Canada. This was because Heinz Ketchup was based in the area since 1909. The company consolidated its operations to the United States and closed its Canadian doors in 2017. This event lead to a dramatic economic downturn for the area. Consequently, the community has welcomed the emergence of a new use for their greenhouse facilities. Aphria (APH-TSX) is based in Leamington. The tomato capital of Canada may now become the cannabis capitals of the world.

That was the past. Now imagine what it might be like if we could beam 200 years in the future and join the crew of a starship such as the Enterprise. Picture cruising up to a planet and meeting a desperate mother with a child afflicted with a debilitating disease such as epilepsy or cancer. Would you empathize and want to help? If you learned this simple natural plant from their own planet could help with little or no harm, would it seem like a sensible solution to suggest using it? When you learn people who use the plant are subject to legal persecution, criminal oppression, social stigma, and shaming would it make you ask why? When you discover the plant is feared because it makes people feel happy and less pain, would that make you scratch your head and ask what? Not even the universe of *Star Trek* could come up with such an absurd scenario. Offscreen, both William Shatner and Patrick Stewart who played Captains Kirk and Jean Luc Picard on the starship Enterprise have taken public stances advocating the use of cannabis. Shatner has said "Oh, I love marijuana. Marijuana is a great thing." And Stewart is an open medical marijuana user. *Star Trek*'s Whoopi Goldberg has created her own cannabis company named Whoopi and Maya, aimed at the niche women's market. It is the perseverance of the facts and public stances by public profiles and more that will help stage the change in making cannabis acceptable in the future.

A consistent message from many sources over time will influence change. High-profile businesspeople, politicians, and medical professionals are adding to the voices and conceding the past century was a shameful mistake. A new message is being reinforced that cannabis is safe, trustworthy, and credible. Today, *Dragons' Den* compadres W. Brett Wilson and Arlene Dickinson have, respectively, invested millions in cannabis companies and become directors of LPs. British billionaire Richard Branson is a loud cannabis advocate. Former US president Barack Obama confessed to inhaling and surviving. Marketing budgets have invested heavily in branding with musicians Willie Nelson, Melissa Etheridge, the children of Bob Marley, and Snoop Dogg. The next breakthrough may well be professional sports.

The fact has not been lost on me that if I had written this book 25 years earlier I would be subject to a $300,000 fine and possible imprisonment. Also, it would have damaged my credibility and I would have faced a lifetime of social stigma. Does that make you scratch your head? Does this book discuss weapons of mass destruction? (Except for exposing the deadly poisonous truth of the tomato, of course.) I am proud if this book in any way adds my voice to the just cause of making cannabis credible. Truthfully, I am more grateful for what cannabis has given me, including the opportunity to write this book.

Like the tomato, cannabis credibility will happen. With time, I believe cannabis will become a normal, accepted plant used by everyday folk without persecution and stigma. Why? Because it makes sense. Because science is teaching us that cannabis is more helpful than harmful. And because I have the audacity to believe the human species can make mistakes, learn from them, and make better choices going forward.

In conclusion, I would like to offer all the best with your stock choices. I truly hope this book helps you experience the excitement of watching your cannabis investment skyrocket to the moon and beyond.

Appendix I: Glossary

Access to Cannabis for Medicinal Purposes Regulations (ACMPR): the regulations authorized by Health Canada to administer medical marijuana

All or none: special handling order for an order to be completely filled or none at all

Ask: also see *offer*; request to sell

At the market: the bid, ask, or last trade price right now

Bid: request to buy

Board lots: a prepackaged bundle of stocks

Bought deal: a type of financing where the brokerage house assumes 100 percent of the risk and uses its own capital to purchase all the securities being issued

Bull market: a stockbroker's term that indicates there are more buyers than sellers over a period of time resulting in higher prices on the market

Canadian Securities Exchange (CSE): a regulated Canadian stock exchange

Cannabichromene (CBC): a cannabinoid that enhances the effect of THC

Cannabidiol (CBD): a cannabinoid that creates sedation and analgesic effects

Cannabigerol (CBG): a cannabinoid with sedative and antibiotic effects

Cannabinoid receptor: sites throughout the brain and body to which cannabinoid binds

Cannabinoid: chemical compound secreted by cannabis flowers

Cannabinol (CBN): a cannabinoid that is mildly psychoactive

Cannabis: a plant with unique properties

Day trade: an order that is killed at the end of the day if not filled

Exchange traded fund (ETF): a financial instrument with a "basket of stocks" through a single security. The basket will presumably reflect the market the same way an index will reflect the overall market. With a basket of stocks, it is similar to a mutual fund, but as a single security it trades like a stock

Fear Of Missing Out (FOMO): an economic theory that suggests stock prices are increasing because of the psychological fear of missing out on an investment. The risk is the stock may not be worth the value it is trading during the phenomena

Halt: stock has stopped trading either by a regulatory authority or by the company

Hybrid: a cross-strain of indica and sativa. Effects will reflect the dominant strain

Indica: a cannabis plant that is CBD dominant

Investment Industry Regulatory Organization of Canada (IIROC): self-regulatory organization for stock exchanges and stockbrokers

Joint: cannabis rolled like a cigarette

Licensed Producers (LP): a cannabis operator authorized by Health Canada

Limit order: setting an exact price to trade

Market capitalization: the total market value of the securities of a company

Market order: trading at the next available price

Market share: the piece of the sector company has captured sales in comparison to the entire industry

Offer: also see *ask*; request to sell

On-stop order (OS): an open order that is triggered by a stop price. There are OS buy orders and OS sell orders and each can either be a limit or market order. They are intended to work as an insurance tool but can be high risk

Open or good 'til cancelled: order placed with a future cancellation date

Poison pill: a defense strategy against a hostile take-over. The company defending the take-over dilutes its stock. By doing so, it makes it more difficult for the aggressing company to acquire shares

Private placement: a small underwriting of securities to a private group of buyers

Registered Retirement Savings Plan (RRSP): a tax avoidance account for investments

Reverse-take-over (RTO): sometimes called a *backdoor listing*. It is a way to take a company public on the stock market without going through the normal detail-oriented process of listing requirements and fees. For example, company A is a cannabis company that wishes to trade on the stock exchange, but as a new venture start up, it wants to save costs where possible. It costs for lawyers, accountants, business analysts, specialists, and administration fees to scrutinize and do the diligence for listing requirements. Company B is a venture mining company who has already paid the costs to be listed on an exchange. Unfortunately, Company B has not struck gold and is running out of money to maintain the listing requirements. Company A buys 50 percent of company B to acquire controlling interest. Then Company A can transfer its assets to Company B. Hence it is take over by a private company of a public company, and that makes it reverse

Sativa: a cannabis plant that is THC dominant

Securities: an investment contract that is transferable. Examples are stocks, bonds, mutual funds, exchange traded funds and derivatives such as rights, warrants, call and put options

Settlement period: the two days it takes for a stock contract to settle

Shake: the stem of the cannabis plant

Shares outstanding: outstanding stocks for a company trading on the market

Special handling: unique trading instructions for the traders to follow

Stock: represents ownership and can be called *equity*, or *shares*

Task force report: a framework for the legalization and regulation of cannabis in Canada presented to parliament November 30, 2016

Tax-Free Savings Account (TFSA): a tax avoidance account for investments

Terpenes: found in most plants and contribute to taste and smell

THC delta-9-tetrahydocannabinol (THC): a cannabinoid that creates euphoria

The Venture Exchange (TSXV): a regulated Canadian stock exchange

Ticker: symbol representing a stock

Toronto Stock Exchange (TSX): a regulated Canadian stock exchange

Appendix II:
Sources and Resources

Cannabis Company Websites

AB Laboratories Inc.
   www.ablabs.ca

ABcann Medicinals
   www.abcann.ca

Aphria
   aphria.com

Aurora
   auroramj.com

Broken Coast Cannabis Ltd.
   brokencoast.ca

Canna Farms
   www.cannafarms.ca

CanniMed
www.cannimed.ca

CannTrust
canntrust.ca

Cronos Group
thecronosgroup.com

Emblem
emblemcannabis.com

Emerald Health Botanicals
www.emerald.care

Ever Green Medicinals
www.evergreenmedicinal.ca

Green Relief
www.greenrelief.ca

Greenleaf Medical Clinic
greenleafmc.ca

Newstrike.
www.newstrike.ca

Hydropothecary
thehydropothecary.com

Invictus
invictus-md.com

Maple Leaf Green World Inc.
www.mlgreenworld.com

Marapharm Ventures
www.marapharm.com

MariCann
www.maricann.com

MedReleaf
medreleaf.com

New Cannabis Ventures Inc.
www.newcannabisventures.com

Organigram
www.organigram.ca

PeaceNaturals
www.peacenaturals.com

Prairie Plant Systems Inc.
prairieplant.com

Redcan
www.redecan.ca

Supreme
www.supreme.ca/home/default.aspx

7Acres
www.7acres.com

Tantalus Labs
tantaluslabs.com

The Green Organic Dutchman
www.tgod.ca

Tilray
www.tilray.ca

THC BioMed Plant Science
thcbiomed.com

TrueLeaf
www.trueleaf.com

Tweed Main Street
www.tweedmainstreet.com

United Greeneries
www.unitedgreeneries.ca

Weed MD
www.weedmd.com

Whistler Medical Marijuana Corporation
whistlermedicalmarijuana.com

Investment Websites

BMO Investor Line
www.bmo.com/investorline/self-directed/

CIBC Investor's Edge
www.investorsedge.cibc.com/en/home.html

National Bank Direct Brokerage
nbdb.ca

Qtrade Investor
www.qtrade.ca/investor

Questrade
www.questrade.com

RBC Direct Investing
www.rbcdirectinvesting.com

Scotia iTrade
www.scotiabank.com/itrade/en/0,,3527,00.html

TD Direct Investing
www.td.com/ca/products-services/investing/
td-direct-investing/index-res.jsp?cm_sp=:MICROSOFT:
General+Branded:DIF:p11539212928

TMX Money
web.tmxmoney.com/getquote.php

TMX Money, Market Activity
www.tmxmoney.com/en/index.html

Articles and Websites of Interest

Akin, David. "Pot's Retail Therapy." *National Post*, accessed April 2018.
news.nationalpost.com/features/0-cannabis-retail-therapy

Berke, Jeremy. "DELOITTE: Legal weed could be a $22.6 billion
industry in Canada." *Business Insider*, October 27, 2016.
www.businessinsider.com/deloitte-weed-could-be-226-
billion-canada-2016-10

Blaszczak-Boxe, Agata. "Marijuana's History: How One Plant
Spread Through the World." *Live Science*, October 17, 2014.
www.livescience.com/48337-marijuana-history-how-cannabis-
travelled-world.html

Brainy Quote. "Tommy Chong." Accessed April, 2018.
www.brainyquote.com/authors/tommy_chong

Butler, Colin. "Canada made marijuana illegal 94 years ago and no
one's sure why." CBC, May 2, 2017.
www.cbc.ca/news/canada/kitchener-waterloo/why-
marijuana-was-made-illegal-canada-mystery-1.4095243

Daily Mail Reporter. "The tomato was feared for 200 YEARS by Europeans who called it 'poison apple' and thought it to be sinful and seductive." *Daily Mail*, June 20, 2013.
www.dailymail.co.uk/news/article-2344845/The-tomato-feared-200-YEARS-Europeans-called-poison-apple-thought-sinful-seductive.html#ixzz5C8WezKhk

Jenkins, Nash. "Scientists Detect Traces of Cannabis on Pipes Found in William Shakespeare's Garden." *TIME*, August 10, 2015.
time.com/3990305/william-shakespeare-cannabis-marijuana-high

Holland, Julie MD. *The Pot Book: A Complete Guide to Cannabis.* Rochester: Park Street Press, 2010.

Lift News
https://news.lift.co/

Marijuana News/420 Intel. "High in Hawaii: Cheech and Chong Talk Marijuana and Donald Trump." 420 Intel, May 6, 2016.
420intel.com/articles/2016/05/06/high-hawaii-cheech-and-chong-talk-marijuana-and-donald-trump

McClure, James. "William Shatner Boldly Goes Where No Talk Show Host Has Gone Before." Civilized, Mar 22, 2016.
www.civilized.life/articles/William-Shatner-marijuana-star-trek

Onder Koffer V. "Cannabis-researcher: "THC for children with cancer." YouTube, April 30, 2017.
www.youtube.com/watch?v=wYJQreAg3DU

Reason TV. "The Science of Medical Cannabis: A conversation with Donald Abrams, MD." YouTube, October 14, 2010.
www.youtube.com/watch?v=IHBsxfbgrbY

Schwartz, Daniel. "Marijuana was criminilized in 1923, but why?" CBC, May 3, 2014.
www.cbc.ca/news/health/marijuana-was-criminalized-in-1923-but-why-1.2630436

Up In Smoke. Wikipedia, accessed April, 2018.
en.wikipedia.org/wiki/Up_in_Smoke

Laws and Other Sources

Health Canada. A Framework for the Legalization and Regulation of Cannabis in Canada. The Final Report of the Task Force on Cannabis Legilization and Regulation. Ottawa: The Government of Canada, 2016. Parliamentary report.

Authorized Licensed Producers for Medical Purposes
www.hc-sc.gc.ca/dhp-mps/marihuana/info/list-eng.php

Canadian Securities Exchange
http://thecse.com/

Investment Industry Regulatory Organization of Canada (IIROC)
www.iiroc.ca/Pages/default.aspx

Government of Canada, "Introduction of the Cannabis Act: Questions and Answers":
https://www.canada.ca/en/services/health/campaigns/
introduction-cannabis-act-questions-answers.html

SEDAR
http://sedar.com

Wikipedia Drug Policy of Canada
https://en.wikipedia.org/wiki/Drug-policy-of-Canada